Praise for *Beyond Becoming*

Almost anyone can gather a group, figure out an activity or even lead a Bible study. When the group is over, have we made any changes that will last – even a year? Stop simply running small groups and start seeing lasting changes for the better. *Beyond Belonging* takes you there.

— **Dr. Jim Wilder, neurotheologian and founder of Life Model Works**

Once again Ed Khouri has written a work that is readily understood and applied. Yet, beneath the surface, it is clear his many years of scholarship and study in how we think and why has been brought to bear. That combination will make this book a must-have for anyone seeking to lead a small group. Yet the most precious thing expressed throughout this masterpiece is his practical determination to encourage us to connect, in real-time, with God together. That, right there, will change you forever!

— **Andy Reese, author, speaker, and president of Freedom Prayer (www.freedomprayer.com)**

In his first book, *Becoming a Face of Grace*, Ed Khouri passionately introduces his readers to creative ways to recognize abundant grace around and within us. Ed helps us become aware of the four *P*s of pleasing, performing, pain, and pleasure that may sidetrack us on the path of authentic discipleship. In this book, *Beyond Becoming*, Ed invites his readers to embrace the startling, life-giving revelation that "eternity starts here and now!" He powerfully guides us through the process of how to build grace-based relationships in community through the four R's where we learn to receive, reflect, repair, and restore. In this way, we mirror the loving unity of our Trinitarian God, who creates, redeems, and sanctifies us and makes all things new! Highly recommend this book for all who seek to grow in grace and build grace-anchored communities.

— **Marijane R. Michalowicz, parish lay minister, volunteer, and associate of the Sisters of St. Joseph**

Ed Khouri's book *Beyond Becoming* is one of the best books written on how to have an effective small group. Based on a biblically sound structure, it is a roadmap to understanding ongoing personal connection with Jesus *first*, as well as how to cultivate deep relationship with others.

— **Pastor John Leach, lead pastor of Jubilee Fellowship Church**

Grace-based small groups are a vital part of Christian discipleship. In *Beyond Becoming* Ed Khouri explains exactly why this is the case. He leads us through the biblical basis for joy-filled relationships in a small group setting and gives practical advice to help us on the journey together. The wisdom and experience that Ed communicates is never overly prescriptive, giving plenty of room for God-given creativity and diversity in how these groups operate. I am excited to see how the truths that Ed unpacks for us will impact individuals, families, churches, and communities around the world.

— Treflyn Lloyd-Roberts, chief executive of Yeldall Christian Centres and general secretary of International Substance Abuse & Addiction Coalition

beyond
becoming

beyond becoming

A FIELD GUIDE TO SUSTAINABLE, TRANSFORMATIONAL COMMUNITIES

Ed Khouri

ILLUMIFY
MEDIA.COM

beyond
becoming

Unless otherwise noted, Scripture quotations are from The New International Version of the Bible, copyright 2018 by Zondervan Publishing. Used by permission, all rights reserved.

Scripture quotations marked (ESV) are from The Holy Bible, English Standard Version® (ESV®), copyright © 2001 by Crossway, a publishing ministry of Good News Publishers. Used by permission. All rights reserved.

Scripture quotations marked (MSG) from The Message. Copyright © by Eugene H. Peterson 1993, 1994, 1995, 1996, 2000, 2001, 2002. Used by permission of Tyndale House Publishers, Inc.

Scripture quotations taken from the (NASB1995®) New American Standard Bible®, Copyright © 1960, 1971, 1977, 1995, 2020 by The Lockman Foundation. Used by permission. All rights reserved. www.lockman.org.

Scripture marked (NKJV) taken from the New King James Version®. Copyright © 1982 by Thomas Nelson. Used by permission. All rights reserved.

The views and opinions expressed in this book are those of the author and do not necessarily reflect the official policy or position of Illumify Media Global.

Published by
Illumify Media Global
www.IllumifyMedia.com
"Let's bring your book to life!"

Library of Congress Control Number: 2021919185

Paperback ISBN: 978-1-955043-31-1
eBook ISBN: 978-1-955043-32-8

Typeset by Art Innovations (http://artinnovations.in/)
Cover design by Bethany C. Moore

Printed in the United States of America

Dedication

To Mickey Evans
who taught me to see the life of Jesus reflected
in the faces of small group members.

Contents

Foreword

I first met Ed Khouri in Medicine Hat, Alberta, Canada, in 2003. My impressions of Ed at that time were threefold. One, I noticed Ed was attentive to the people around him. He noticed what was going on with people, and he was deeply caring. Two, Ed demonstrated courage to try new things—and stay relational in the process. Ed seemed to have an insatiable curiosity, which drove him to pursue solutions to complex problems. Three, Ed had incredible wisdom. I quickly learned to pay attention to what Ed had to say. I always see the world through a new and refreshing lens when I soak in his writings.

It has been a joy to work with Ed and watch as he writes books, develops curriculum, and trains people around the globe. When Ed asked if I would consider writing the foreword for *Beyond Becoming*, I jumped at the opportunity! My respect for Ed and his work has only increased exponentially over the nearly twenty years I have known him. It is my firm belief you will be influenced as well as inspired by the gold found in *Beyond Becoming*. Here we have a splendid masterpiece detailing steps to develop essentials for lasting transformation that grows in the gardens of our communities. *Beyond Becoming* is the follow-up resource to Ed's previous book, *Becoming a Face of Grace: Navigating Lasting Relationships with God and Others*.

In *Beyond Becoming*, we find the language as well as the framework to take our small groups to a new level. Using a relational lens, years of experience, and personal stories, Ed gives us key ingredients for transformational discipleship where people become genuine apprentices of Jesus who live in grace and love others well. The examples Ed shares put the concepts into action in creative ways the reader can apply. There is so much richness in this book! Ed gives us a practical, achievable resource, a manual we can use, to grow mature leaders who model stable, joy-filled leadership.

Let's be clear. This kind of leadership doesn't happen by chance, nor does it grow from good intentions or more information. Ed tells us we can create sustainable spiritual practices our small groups can use to nourish the soil so that good things grow. Ed provides structure to establish the context where small group leadership and fellowship thrive. Every church leader, every small group, and every person interested to see spiritual communities succeed must read this book! With keen insight, Ed encourages us to practice the activities first before using them with our small groups.

It is possible for leaders to become models of grace that is lived out in our faces and through our interactions. *Beyond Becoming* is the sweet invitation to dive deep into a journey filled with the joyful transformation that defines authentic fellowship. In the close, deep connections with our community and small group friends, we can become the people God intended us to be, or, as Ed puts it, "our relationships help us to find our true selves again" (21). Ed shows us we have the potential to change how we do small groups, how we do community, and how we share life together.

Ed deepens our understanding of grace and puts grace-based discipleship into action through a relational lens where we rely on the people in our lives to see us as God sees us. Our community is the foundational ingredient for lasting transformation! I appreciate how Ed unpacks the biblical relevance of small group ministry along with the language and lens for creating grace-filled small groups that take on the character of Jesus in both word and action. Ed gives us the framework to carve out a path to form small groups that develop transformation zones where Jesus-like character shines.

As Ed explains, "Our grace-based attachments rooted in love are the foundation for everything concerning life, relationships, discipleship, and transformation" (10). Just imagine a world where this reality brings people together and prepares hearts to receive the life Jesus invites us into. Ed tells us we should not look to our leaders to simply carry us through our spiritual lives; we must pause and consider some of the inadequate perspectives that need to be updated and refined—even thrown out. "The responsibility to help create and heal attachments and identity issues falls on each of us—not just the pros. It is an assignment you and I share: *we* are agents of grace" (22). This is a breath of fresh air: *every one of us plays a pivotal role in the process of communities becoming more like Christ.*

In this vital work, we discover essentials for grace-based fellowship where small groups are alive, transformational, and profoundly impactful. Group time focuses on relationships and not simply content, or, as Ed puts it, "fellowship, more than anything else, is a gateway to spiritual growth" (48). I believe it is impossible to read this book and not develop the insatiable longing for a deep dive into grace-based small groups where Jesus is present and people are alive! I couldn't put this book down. Nor could I wait to put it into action with my community.

Ed gives us real answers, real hope, and real perspective to create what he refers to as the "staying power" in our small groups, where we put *the Four Amazing R's* of Relational Grace-based Attachment into action to grow in our awareness of God's peaceful presence. Here, we empower one another to share the good stuff and be more like Christ. All of us can "find shoes that fit," referring to activities based on our personality, gifts, style, and character. In this way, we lead in a way that matches who God intends us to be. All I can say, dear reader, is this: welcome to the journey—it has the potential to change how you do kingdom life and build kingdom relationships.

— Chris M. Coursey
President of THRIVEtoday
Author of *The Joy Switch: How Your Brain's Secret Circuit Affects Your Relationships—And How You Can Activate It*

Acknowledgments

The Beatles' classic "A Little Help from my Friends" captures how I feel. Much like music, *Beyond Becoming* has a rhythm and melody written for those eager to grow more deeply connected with God and each other together in grace. Thanks to the input and patience of many, we've been able to avoid the sour notes so that you are able to enjoy the sweet sound of fellowship as you use this book together. Specifically, I'd like to thank the following:

My wife, Maritza, who is my number one sounding board for ideas. Her help is, as always, invaluable.

The Life Group Leaders at New Life Church in Taylorsville, North Carolina, who have listened patiently in training sessions and have proven through years of leadership that the concepts and exercises you are about to learn create environments rich with grace, God's presence, and transformational fellowship.

My friend Jim Wilder, who provided valuable encouragement and support, especially when I had difficulty hitting the right notes when writing.

As with *Becoming a Face of Grace*, this book would simply not be possible without the incredible work of Amy Pierson. Working from my notes, recordings, outlines, PowerPoint presentations, and numerous video conferences, Amy helped me craft the work you now hold. She also assisted with editing my initial drafts and made countless suggestions that make this work stronger, clearer, and more readable. Amy is a genius at knowing exactly when I need to tell a story! She helped make this work much more "user-friendly" than I would have accomplished on my own. I am deeply grateful to her and find working with her to be a true joy.

To the writers and musicians whose sounds and lyrics I love so much and who have inspired the "unforced rhythms of grace" (Matthew 11:28–30 MSG), from deep in my soul, thank you for the love, discipleship, and relationships you've enriched in my life. My heart sings with gratitude for each of you.

Introduction
and How to Use This Book

God is not just saving individuals and preparing them for heaven; rather, He is creating a people among whom He can live and who in their life together will reproduce God's life and character. This view of salvation is consistent throughout Paul's letters.

—GORDON FEE

You know those days after a long, gray winter when you can taste springtime? The earthy warmth and wafts of blossoms in the breeze wake something up inside us all. It was that kind late-April day in Maryland, 1985. As a member of law enforcement at the time, I found it to be the kind that breeds a fever for freedom in high school kids. Crazed and fully afflicted, a carload of them left the school parking lot headed for lunchtime liberty, packed into an overstuffed Ford Escort. Jared was the young driver behind the wheel. I got to know him as part of an accident investigation that day.

The young man's quickest route to the Sonic was down a long, precipitous hill laden with curves. To this day, I'm not sure if he was distracted by all the chatter or encountered some unexpected g-forces along the way, but, whatever happened, it didn't end well. Without question, the speed Jared was traveling was not safe for anyone. Yaw marks and skid tracks told the story of a car sliding sideways—first one way, overcorrecting, and then another—before slamming into a guardrail. Careening into the guardrail was preferable to plummeting over the deep ditch it protected them from; however, the force of their impact caused the hatchback to unhinge. One young man was ejected and badly hurt.

First to respond with me was another cop who was also a Christian. As we helped paramedics move the injured teen over the guardrail, the two of us were able to pray over him. Needless to say, it was uniquely traumatic for Jared, the injured boy, and all the rest of the passengers. Nobody meant for the accident to happen, yet you could almost see it coming.

In nearly forty years of leading, developing, and creating new approaches to small groups, I've noted similar perils on the road to discipleship. Jared's accident is an apt metaphor for what happens to many leaders and churches. That is,

- We gather a group and think it's all downhill (simple, right?).
- We go too fast in what is the slow process of discipleship.
- Our speed sends us sideways, and we often overcorrect as a reaction.
- People sometimes get hurt—as our groups hurl into ditches or guardrails.

Let's face it, it is important that we stay on the road to discipleship, but how do we stay in our small group lane? In my experience, most start off with good intentions but too many encounter bumps that send them veering off course. Before they know it, they get stuck in a ditch. To better understand, let's consider some aspects of healthy small groups versus the hazards that lay in the ditches.

ASPECTS OF HEALTHY SMALL GROUPS	DITCHES ON THE DISCIPLESHIP ROAD
Solid Bible study	Passive listeners who don't engage with Scripture for themselves
Strong sense of accountability among leaders and members	Abuses that lead to control, narcissism, and fear-based conformity
Growth in support and recovery groups as members share struggles and experiences with life-controlling problems	Inability to empower group members to engage with broader church in community
Authenticity as groups gather to share personal pain, problems, and prayer	Group becomes a problem-focused dumping ground for personal pain, dominated by negativity, gossip, and toxicity

These are just a sampling that I've noticed on the road. Sadly, too often, small groups pull out of one ditch, overcorrect, and end up in another. Or worse, church leadership gets so frustrated that they give up on the concept of small groups altogether. Instead, they replace them with a pastor-led Bible study (which has limited potential for lasting spiritual transformation). But Jesus' way of making disciples and modeling discipleship accepts no substitutes. Done His way, both require "doing life together." Groups without opportunity for grace-based interaction are no improvement at all.

Perhaps our leaders just need driving lessons? If you and I are on the road to discipleship, church is our proverbial "driver's ed"—where we go to learn about the privileges, strategies, rules, hazards, and consequences to help us stay out of these ditches.

THE LOCAL CHURCH: CONTEXT FOR *BEYOND BECOMING*

I am a firm believer in the importance of the local church. Without it, my calling and what you are reading have no context. For more than fifteen years, I've been solidly rooted as both a member and an elder at New Life Church in Taylorsville, North Carolina. I've spent more than forty years creating small group models and training leaders around the world. So when our church leadership team approached me five years ago and asked me to develop a new, biblically based small group ministry for our church, I jumped at the opportunity. I knew before I started that the leader training would be key too. What I had in mind was simple but would be an entirely new way of doing things. We were all eager to get started!

Based on a foundation of grace-based discipleship, what developed is the model you will discover in this book.[1] Several months into the work, I began testing the new concepts with two training groups. One group consisted of leaders from outside our church community, and the other group contained potential small group leaders from within our church. Since launching small groups a few years ago, the response has been amazing. All the stories you will read in this book come from our leadership test groups—or my life experience. I'm happy to report that this model is working—and I invite you to join us in this new way of being.

THREE CONVICTIONS THAT GUIDE MY APPROACH TO SMALL GROUP LEADERSHIP

If I ran this "driving school," we would operate around three convictions that experience has rutted in the roads of my small group discipleship philosophy:

1. **Jesus' command to "go and make disciples of all nations" is as on fire as ever.** (Matthew 28:19-20) Discipleship is nothing new—even Jesus didn't invent it (though he did refine the art). In His day, many leading rabbis had disciples—these apprentices lived so close to their master that they were said to be covered in the dust kicked up as their masters walked. The highly relational experience taught them to see, be and do like their masters.

2. **The framework of a small group is only as good as its foundation.** In road building, the building that happens during this foundational phase is called earthwork. A roadway with substandard foundation work (earthwork) is doomed to fall, eventually. Because these proper base layers are as important as the road's surface, the initial grating, leveling, filling, and drainage must be done well. In essence, the earthwork of small group discipleship all comes down to grace (for more on the subject, see my previous book, *Becoming a Face of Grace*). Establishing a firm, clear, and explicit grace-based foundation creates a basis for your small group to travel on—one ready to accommodate many unique routes to a with-God life.

3. **Creative diversity is necessary for thriving small group discipleship.** When it comes to small groups, one size never fits all! God is simply too big for cookie-cutter expressions of

His heart. Our groups must be flexible enough to reflect His care and to disciple different types of people at the same time. When it comes to the design of individual small groups, no two need to be the same.

THREE ESSENTIAL FOUNDATIONS WE WILL BUILD UPON

In *Beyond Becoming*, we will travel the road of grace-based discipleship onward from what was described in my previous book, *Becoming a Face of Grace*. The "manual" ahead will help you learn a new model of leadership and develop spiritual practices to grow a wide variety of small groups. I recommend building three essential foundations into every small group gathering:

1. Offering and receiving grace
2. Experiencing God's presence
3. Practicing activities that focus our attention on the "things above" described in Colossians 3. These activities are pivotal to helping us intentionally connect more deeply with the life of God—and share that life. (Each activity is simple enough to do in your everyday life as well.)

THREE PARTS—HOW THE BOOK IS ORGANIZED

You will notice *Beyond Becoming* is divided into three parts:

- **Part 1** establishes a solid scriptural foundation for this approach to small group ministry.
- **Part 2** offers detailed instructions for seven *Beyond Becoming* activities to help you grow grace in your small group setting. Each activity includes the following:
  - A story that illustrates how to apply the activity in everyday situations
  - The biblical basis for the activity
  - Detailed instructions for leading the activity

- o A personal story from a group member describing the impact of that activity in their life
- Finally, **Part 3** describes ways you can unleash your creativity to make your small group your own.

BETTER, NOT PERFECT

I want to be really clear: the small group model put forth in these pages is built on a better foundation, but it's not perfect. Perfect groups and perfect leaders are as common as unicorns and flying horses. However, I strongly believe the convictions, foundations, and activities contained in these pages set up a better discipleship process than what most of us are familiar with—one rooted in the transformative relationships that will successfully support it.

In our church community, despite our various shortcomings, our leaders, their group members, and I are all growing as Jesus' apprentices. With the help of what we learned in the development of this process, I believe that growth is easier than ever before. Responding out of grace-based relationship with one another and practicing activities that facilitate this kind of relationship enables leaders and group members to increasingly reflect on and experience God's presence.

As a developer and teacher, I have created numerous handouts, PowerPoint presentations, recordings, and notes to use with my classes and groups over the years. Knowing that when groups multiply so does the workload, this material has been streamlined to make it easier to train leaders and launch new small groups. *Beyond Becoming* is designed to help leaders create and build a simple structure and activities necessary for life-giving, grace-based discipleship groups. I recommend that anyone wanting to lead a group based upon this book master the activities they want to use before trying them out on members. Personal practice allows leaders to discover new creative freedom as they build dynamic groups.

SOME FINAL PRACTICAL THOUGHTS BEFORE YOU BEGIN

Keep in mind that this is not intended to be a "one and done" venture. Please don't race through these pages and skip over the benefits of personal practice. A richer spiritual life and more effective leadership are at stake. Because you are both a leader and a disciple, you are a model of grace to those in your care. As Jesus' apprentices, all disciples deserve well-trained leaders who can facilitate the dynamics of His presence with others. If you haven't already, I'd encourage you to take time to read *Becoming a Face of Grace* and consider leading a group through it. Practice the Scripture Reflection activity. As you do, try your best to stay relational and full of grace.

If you are a small group ministry supervisor, build your training process carefully—including the selection of small group leaders. In every interaction you have with small groups and small group leaders, make grace your goal. Going forward, consider how you can continue meeting with your leaders and supervising their activities to keep things out of the ditch. Again, all of these steps take time and careful consideration.

GOING BEYOND

I have no doubt that you will go beyond what you've previously experienced of God's grace. I'm excited by the depths of grace I continue to discover on my own journey as well as the abundant creativity and passion He has placed in the leaders He has called in groups I've led and observed. Their hearts express His. It has been my joy to watch them work. I'm sure your heart will do the same.

PART 1

FOUNDATIONAL BIBLICAL PRINCIPLES FOR SMALL GROUP MINISTRY

1

To Infinity and Beyond: An Overview of Grace

10, 9, ignition sequence start, 6, 5, 4, 3, 2, 1, zero. All engines running. Liftoff! We have a liftoff! Thirty-two minutes past the hour. Liftoff on Apollo 11!

—JACK KING, NASA CHIEF
OF PUBLIC INFORMATION

There was a time when no one ever thought we could do things like send a man to the moon, beat a four-minute mile, or break the sound barrier. There are limits, after all, right? But just when we are all settled into our assumptions, some yahoo shows up to push the envelope.

Jesus was one of those. He pushed the religious envelope of his day and, I daresay, every button of those who thought they had the rules down. He went beyond the man-made limits to bust the system in the greatest, albeit nonsensical, exchange of all time: His perfect life for ours. But why?

All for the sake of grace, it seems.

WHAT IS GRACE?

First, let's just put it out there: God's grace-based vision is mind-boggling. "Who can know it?" Scripture says (Romans 11:33–34 NIV). It spans eternity and scans the heart of each of us—His dear ones. On most days, the idea that the Lord of all would desire your company or mine is inconceivable. Despite ourselves, He evidently knows something we do not.

Superheroes just *know*, don't they? (Of course they do, or else they'd just be super*normals*). Instead of living within natural limits, they do supernatural things. Take *Toy Story*'s Buzz Lightyear, for example. Did you know he was a theologian? That's right. Before jetting off to save the world (or someone therein), the space ranger action figure is known to proudly proclaim, "To infinity and beyond!"

Infinity is an idea with no physical boundaries, no sensible way to "work it out"—a concept concocted by mathematicians to confound mere mortals like you and me. In reality, grace goes beyond natural limits to save us, too, and the King of Kings is far more than a superhero. A *real* gift from God to us, his grace goes beyond infinity-busting. It has no limits. Outside the logical frontiers of movies, comic books, or even our amazing brains, grace extends its unsearchable goodness for all eternity. While it may not be easy to grasp the Lord's reasoning, a primary step into this spiritual space only requires that we understand that, like gravity, grace just *is*.

In order to bring things down to Earth, let's review what we know about God's grace.

THE GIFT OF A PERSONAL INVITATION

Both now and always, grace is a personal invitation. You see, at the time *charis* (the Greek word for "grace") originated, it denoted a pair of inextricably joined ideas; by definition, early Christians understood that grace was part unmerited *gift* and part *invitation* to ongoing, reciprocal relationship. The two could not be separated. Scholars tell us that in those days, receiving a charis from another was far more significant than just getting an undeserved present. For starters, only a person of higher position could extend a gift of grace to someone lower than they were. Back in the day, the favor being extended was obvious to everyone. But what made the offering such a big deal was the motivation of the grace giver. If you offered such a grace to me, we were both clear of your interest and intention; offering a charis expressed that you were inviting me to pursue a deep, mutual, and ongoing relationship. By receiving your grace gift, I would have been expressing my life-long commitment to pursue the same. From that time on, we would have become staunchly and mutually devoted to one another's good.

Many of us have heard grace explained as God's "unmerited favor." Yes, and true. Clearly, it *is* unearned, and He was doing us a favor. Despite the personal *de*merits of our old life, this definition emphasizes the relational jump start we—who are otherwise undeserving—have been given. This is not a misunderstanding of grace, just an incomplete definition.

Regardless of what you've been taught up to now, it is generally agreed that grace benefits and redeems all who love Christ, affording each of us a whole new life in Him. But hopefully, understanding the cultural context of Jesus' time, now you can see grace in its full scope: fully expressed, grace is an unmerited invitation to the gift of redemptive, reciprocal relationship with a God who sees us as far greater than we see ourselves. It is God's means of *starting* a relationship with you and me. Our Charis-Giver God knows that grace-based time with Him—both alone and with others on the spiritual journey—will inspire the life change for which our hearts long.

Because of grace, you and I can claim the words of Galatians 2:20–21 as our own: "I have been crucified with Christ and I no longer live, but Christ lives in me. The life I now live in the body, I live by faith in the Son of God, who loved me and gave himself for me. I do not set aside the grace of God, for if righteousness could be gained through the law, Christ died for nothing!"

When you or I accept this personal, unmerited invitation to follow Jesus, we lay down our lives to "become Christian." Christ's death purchased our ticket, and it's time to get on board. Our destination is guaranteed: we can look forward to spending the rest of eternity getting to know and enjoy life with Him. Depending on where you're coming from, that may or may not sound like a place you want to go. As Dallas Willard notes, "I believe that the only people who will not be in heaven are people who don't want to be there. When you think about it, if you don't really like God, you don't want to be in heaven."[2] Not only does this gift afford us eternity with the gift giver who loves us and sent Jesus, but it also transforms everything about us! Limiting our understanding of grace to merely a "gift" misses the second aspect of grace.

As covered in *Becoming a Face of Grace*,

[A] good number of sincere followers of Jesus have unintentionally been operating under a functional—but reduced—theology that centers on grace as it relates to salvation. While this is important, coming at grace this way effectively limits the practical power and application of it in our everyday life with God. This limited understanding of grace dumbs down life with God; effectively, all the rich marrow is sucked from our spiritual bones.[3]

Eternity starts here and now! Don't miss it. Grace is so much more than unmerited favor. To receive the grace of God through Jesus means accepting that God has a boundless capacity of relational grace toward us as well as toward every other person we meet (and we all know we all need it!). Do you have a habit of looking at other people through this sort of generous, grace-based lens? Because of His capacity, God can honestly see each person as his most special and favorite, times infinity. No limits.

If God has that capacity, and you and I are created in his image, then we each have the same potential to become faces of grace to others once we have responded to His invitation. When you and I encounter, experience, and grow in God's relational grace, it will be reflected in our lives. Learning to see through eyes of grace shows on our faces as we relate with the people around us. Today more than ever, this is the face and grace-filled vision that you and I need to reflect in the world. At the core, it will change how we do life in community—especially in our families, our small groups, and our close friendships. As Paul wrote to the Corinthians, everything about how we view others changes in light of God's grace:

> Because of this decision, we don't evaluate people by what they have or how they look. We looked at the Messiah that way once and got it all wrong, as you know. We certainly don't look at him that way anymore. Now we look inside, and what we see is that anyone united with the Messiah gets a fresh start, is created new. The old life is gone; a new life emerges! Look at it! All this comes from the God who settled the relationship between us and him, and then called us to settle our relationships with each other. God put the world square with himself through the Messiah, giving the world a fresh start by offering forgiveness of sins. (2 Corinthians 5:16–18 MSG)

God no longer sees us according to our old way of being . . . we are new creations! This translation underscores the bottom line: God settled it. Part and parcel to His grace, He says each person you meet is extraordinary—worth the life of His Son, in fact. His special and favorite, that's you and that's me. Get it, and everything about the way we relate with one another will change. At the risk of overstating the obvious, the grace you receive is meant to be shared . . . and don't be surprised if for some it is their first true encounter with grace.

When you and I encounter Jesus and discover His presence among us, it doesn't mean that we blindly accept sin or cheapen the idea of loving one another by unconditionally glossing over weaknesses. Quite to the contrary, it means that *because* of God's grace and loving-kindness toward you and me, we can respond to imperfections and momentary malfunctions as He would.

The words of 2 Corinthians 12:9–10 (NASB1995) are instructive: "And He has said to me, 'My grace is sufficient for you, for power is perfected in weakness.' Most gladly, therefore, I will rather boast about my weaknesses, so that the power of Christ may dwell in me. Therefore I am well content with weaknesses, with insults, with distresses, with persecutions, with difficulties, for Christ's sake; for when I am weak, then I am strong."

What a relief it would be if you and I could experience *and* offer this to one another within our faith communities. Naturally, this is God's intention for us. In his famous book *A Hidden Wholeness: The Journey Toward an Undivided Life,* sociologist Parker Palmer, brilliantly describes the gentleness and patience with which we must approach our souls and the souls of others.

> The soul is like a wild animal—tough, resilient, savvy, self-sufficient and yet exceedingly shy. If we want to see a wild animal, the last thing we should do is to go crashing through the woods, shouting for the creature to come out. But if we are willing to walk quietly into the woods and sit silently for an hour or two at the base of a tree, the creature we are waiting

for may well emerge, and out of the corner of an eye we will catch a glimpse of the precious wildness we seek.[4]

God's grace empowers us to sit quietly with ourselves and one another, so we become brave enough to be seen out in the open. Wild things that we are, if you and I love one another—in good times and bad, through our best behavior and our foibles—you and I will demonstrate His faithful presence as well as our own.

This reminds me of a nature encounter I had on a trip to Montana a few years ago. There, sweeping spaces are interrupted only by mountains that slice their way skyward out of valley floors. (If you saw the movie *A River Runs Through It*, starring a baby-faced Brad Pitt, I don't need to say more.) Big Sky Country is like Narnia for nature lovers. That being us, my wife, Maritza, and I have stayed in a cabin there many times. One early morning, just like C. S. Lewis's heroine Lucy being drawn to step through the wardrobe, I found myself tugged outside and quietly padding a trail alone in search of wildlife. V-e-r-y slowly and deliberately, I took each step—leading with my heel, trying not to snap twigs as my weight shifted forward. To my right stretched a wide-open meadow, and on my left were woods that became increasingly dense as the ground rolled higher up the hill. I could scarcely hear my breath. I like to think that I would have made a great game tracker on the Western frontier.

I'd gone about 150 yards when it happened. I looked up, and there sharing my silence stood a majestic bull elk about twenty feet away in the woods. He was busy enjoying his breakfast. We locked eyes for a moment, and as I exhaled, he went back to grazing. It was kind of magical. Every so often, he'd glance at me again between bites. Head in the grass, the elk slowly worked his way through the woods parallel to my path. Keeping my distance and a good number of trees between us, I walked silently farther down the path. Seemingly unconcerned, the elk would occasionally stop eating and look up at me. When eventually he wandered out of sight into a dense grove of trees, I thought it best to turn back (I didn't want to surprise another, *less* friendly form of wildlife). Honestly, I probably shouldn't have been out there alone. With that in mind, I made plenty of noise as I headed back to our cabin for my own breakfast.

My adventure in the wild highlights what Palmer alludes to: our souls need "elk space." Everyone can learn from adventures on the trail. If we are to join one another in the wild, we must create conditions that invite each other out in the open. In that space, we can best observe, invite, and companion one another through the forest.

ATTACHMENT: GRACE-BASED OR OTHERWISE

Those with whom we share the closest relational connections have the greatest impact on our behavior. We call these deep, enduring, and close relationships "attachments." That is to say, who we love determines how we behave. These relationships powerfully shape our lives and behavior to determine our identity, our personality, our brain's development, and the function of our central nervous system. That is why who—or what—I *love* is more important to my discipleship than what I *know*. Our grace-based attachments rooted in love are the foundation for everything concerning life, relationships, discipleship, and transformation. Jesus talks about the relationship between attachment and obedience like this:

> As the Father has loved me, so have I loved you. Now remain in my love. If you keep my commands, you will remain in my love, just as I have kept my Father's commands and remain in his love. I have told you this so that my joy may be in you and that your joy may be complete. My command is this: Love each other as I have loved you. Greater love has no one than this: to lay down one's life for one's friends. (John 15:9–13)

In this passage, the verb tense for *love* is important to note. Here, the word *love* is telling us that we are to love and *keep on loving*. Jesus does not say, "Love one another . . . for now," "Love . . . unless you just can't anymore," or ". . . until something better comes along." What He says is if we want to remain in His and the Father's love, we must obey the call: "Love and keep on loving as I have . . . lay down your life for your friends." His model of enduring, grace-based love promises a yield of completed joy.

The ramifications of this truth are weighty . . . and the evidence is everywhere. Especially as it pertains to our faith journey, attachment is what keeps us in the sheepfold (John 10:11–18) or—if you'd like another image from Scripture—helps us stay attached to the vine (John 15:4–11). As a response to the grace of God, this place of attachment is where each of us belongs.

Grace-based joyful attachments with others optimize these connections as we grow—making our relationships with God and others "sticky" and full of love. In God's grand scheme of things, how we attach to Him and others has more influence over the formation of our character than anything else. Put another way: who or what we love shapes our lives and behavior more powerfully than anything. So who do you love most? These loves will *always* trump good information, effective teaching, or "how-to" books on living the Christian life. We hunger for connection, not information. As a result, if as C. S. Lewis wrote, "Every Christian is to become a little Christ," we need one another in the process.[5] Well attached to Jesus and one another, grace-driven transformation all boils down to love, changes everything about us, and releases God's influence into the world around us.

Did you learn that in Sunday school (or whatever context led you to Jesus)? Or did that get left out of the script, like it was for me? Whatever your story, if you want to grow spiritually, prioritize time to connect genuinely with God and other people.

This simple idea is the launchpad for spiritual transformation. You see, in the end we aren't just calculating conversions here; if you and I want to see lives—our own and others'—formed to be like Jesus in sustainable, grace-filled ways, this is the only route. To help us navigate the change, two basic elements are required:

- Ongoing personal interactions with Jesus
- Grace-filled, flexible, ongoing relationships with others

Grab this, and there is no going back: grace, discipleship, and maturity depend on these things. In John 10, Jesus addresses our need for his guidance and relationship when He calls us his "sheep." Unlike Buzz Lightyear, sheep do not have superpowers. In fact, some would call them dumb. They are herd animals that go where their shepherd calls them . . . together. Not only do they listen to the shepherd's voice, but they also have the innate sense that there is safety in numbers. (Do you know what a sheep standing alone in a field is called? Lunch.) As you and I interact more with Jesus and one another, we will discover a robust meaning and provision of grace and as a result our true identity will grow. So, prepare to launch!

Grace, attachment, and love all speak to the essential longing within each of us to connect with both God and others. Experiencing the Lord's grace together will take us places beyond our wildest expectations of faith. With that in mind, journey onward. Buzz Lightyear would be proud!

2 *Small Groups as Family*

The saint burns grace like a 747 burns fuel.

—DALLAS WILLARD

God designed our natural family to be the place where you and I learn to live in grace. Drawing on what we now know about grace helps each of us better understand His intention for grace in the context of our spiritual families too. For those who have received Jesus, family is a space where relationships remain bigger and more important than our problems. Here, grace can form bonds, attachments, and identity in the good ways that you and I need. Unfortunately, the family that raises us can also be a place where *bad* things happen. That being the case, you can count on it: the grace you and I experience through family interactions has been—and will be—formed and tested through good times and stormy, alike. Grace points to a profound relational need—a reciprocal one. Each of us is born with it. Naturally, that need is magnified in families.

NO FAIRY TALE

Made up of imperfect people, family life is no fairy tale. Sometimes we can get pretty off the plotline God would prefer. Though we may love the characters in our own, families can be a mess (granted, some more than others). Thanks to the personal sin, iniquity, and transgression inbred in the legacy of our lives, there aren't as many happy endings as God would like. Though fairy tales seem to work out well for most princes and princesses, let's be honest: the majority of the time, the roots of said protagonists are generally just as whacked as our own. I mean, really, who

- sends their two young kids into the woods with a loaf of bread and no warnings about hot ovens, witches, and stranger danger?
- hightails it out of a haunted castle to save himself, leaving his beautiful daughter in a beast's dungeon?
- kills off her stepdaughter with a poison apple just so she can be "the fairest in the land"?

MESSY

Consider what happened in the perfection of the garden. The first family tested things. Under the most superb circumstances, they experienced a delightful everyday relationship with God. And then—*BAM!*—Adam and Eve slid out of the ideal with a snake. Instead of unspoiled divine connection, in their judgment the couple chose what they thought would be a better way for themselves. Exposed, their fickle relationship with God and one another quickly spiraled into excuses and blame. And let's not even mention the kids. Their storybook strolls with God forever changed course, and it affected all who came after.

Don't forget, that's us! You and I descended from their lineage.

THE FOUR AMAZING R's OF RELATIONAL, GRACE-BASED ATTACHMENT

Obviously, families reflected in Scripture, in fairy tales, and in real-life families of origin today don't mirror God's best garden-born vision. Still, close relationship with grace-filled people is the ideal the

Lord holds before us. In his "big idea," God created our natural family to help powerfully shape our identity and attachment through the Four Amazing R's of Relational, Grace-Based Attachment (from now on, these will be referred to as the Four Amazing R's). Our families help each of us learn what it means to accomplish four vital tasks:

- **Receive** our identity as God's special and favorite (not perfect) child. When we are infants, the people we interact with most demonstrate to us that we have value. There is something in their faces. In the first two years of life particularly, we receive the message from these people, "I'm somebody important, I matter, I am worthy," or we don't.

- **Reflect** to other people that they are a delight too. Sometime between six and nine months old, babies begin to mirror back what they have received. If a little one's sense of attachment and identity is rooted in experiences that tell them they are special, worthy, and welcome, they will smile and grin at just about anyone once they're comfortable. Their adorable little face will amplify joy to almost anyone around. In effect, an internalized sense of their delightfulness has taught them to become a little face of grace in the world.

- **Repair** the breach that will happen when circumstances, choices, mean people, etc. cause attachments or identity to be shaken. When our family reminds us that we are not alone and that we still have value, you and I will be able to return to a secure sense of self. (Spoiler alert: you and I will need to be reminded more than once.) Generally, repair is learned in our family of origin—the ones with whom we already share a grace-based bond. We must have sufficient real relationship with another to form and repair broken attachment. It is less likely in a large extended family setting. Repair helps fix our ability to see one another with eyes of grace.

- **Restore** ruptured grace-based attachments to a healthy state. When a conflict occurs, you and I will need to reconnect to our grace-based attachments in order to reconnect with our individual and group identity. The restoration process helps us return to seeing life through eyes of grace and joy—as God does. Both repair and restore are things that happen best in the context of strong grace-based attachment.

Beyond important, the Four Amazing R's are vital to forming and sustaining a healthy attachment with God and others. For those of us who have relatively healthy family units, their nurture makes it much easier to believe, receive, and share God's grace later in life. These loving bonds and attachments form face-to-face, over time—to become the context for a healthy identity to grow. God knew it from the start. Close connection with family affords you and me our first opportunity to learn the sparkling truth about ourselves (that we are His special and favorite, remember?). Family-forged attachments are essential to our emotional, physical, mental, and spiritual development.

So, if you came from a well-bonded family of origin, congratulations! What a praiseworthy foundation your parents have laid in your life. Though all of us have "gaps," you are way ahead thanks to them. If, however, you're like more than 50 percent of people, the blessing of a stable family base has not been so evenly poured (and sadly, the numbers are trending negative in younger generations). When that is the case, identity and attachments are stunted. Information, social media, online communities, books, TV, movies, or music are no substitute for the deep relational connections we each lack. People's feelings *will* get hurt;

they *will* occasionally get offended. Whichever side you're on, things go wrong—even in the most solid family settings, like the Scotts':

Tom and Lisa Scott live outside Raleigh in a modest family neighborhood with their three children: Luke, Sara, and Haley. Tom is the primary breadwinner, working in upper management for a biotech company. Lisa continues her work as a nutritionist but has cut back to part-time; this way, she can still help with some of the household expenses but manage the day-to-day "shuttle service" to after-school activities, homework supervision, and other domestic demands. The family has prioritized attending their church's Sunday service as well as a midweek youth group for the kids and Bible study for Mom and Dad. As is true in many families, to say the Scotts are stretched for time seems like a gross understatement.

One particular night, Tom left the office with his briefcase overstuffed with paperwork. The hours since he left the house that morning had been exceptionally taxing. Some VIPs from corporate had been in, making it almost impossible to get to the reports he was supposed to present to them the next day. As the garage door went up, so did the tension coiled in the pit of his stomach. Tom walked in the door to hear Lisa in a parenting moment with their middle child: "What do you mean your semester depends on it, Sara? Then why am I *just* hearing about it now?" If you were able to dodge the dagger-eyed glares, you could cut the adolescent tension with a knife.

Great, Tom thought. *Here we go again. I've got too much work tonight. I don't have time for this.* Without stopping to put down his briefcase or pick up the specifics involved, he barked at Sara, "I'm sick of your irresponsibility, kid! You shirk chores and homework, and your sense of entitlement is a pain to be around. Just *once,* could you think of someone besides yourself and be responsible for your own life?"

Ouch. The searing words left Sara teary and defeated—far from feeling like anybody's special and favorite child. Tom had lost track of his own identity along the way too; overwhelmed by the work still ahead that evening, he hated his job and himself now more than ever.

In various forms, this kind of stuff happens to everybody once in a while. Circumstances pile up, fear creeps in, emotions boil over. We snap. The intensity of the problem within the family becomes greater than the dynamics of grace. Once it does, you and I go temporarily grace-blind—we can't see others in the same grace-based way we would like (or at least know we should).

GRACE AND SPIRITUAL FAMILIES

Maneuvering through life, each of us will experience times when we question our identity and where we belong; our bonds and attachments will get rocked. During such moments when our families fail us (and they will), we all want answers that have been unavailable at home. The good news is that the Four Amazing R's don't just apply within our families of origin; they apply in our spiritual families as well.

It seems obvious when you think about it. In Jesus, you and I are part of one big grace-filled household: God's. Built together, we abide in a communal dwelling with him. A welcoming door is always open for each of us, and forever we have a place at the table. Crossing the threshold, you and I will find relational grace in residence; apart from the context of relationships with one another, it can't be known. Ephesians 2:17–22 (ESV), makes it plain: literally, God purposed that you and I be part of his ever-spiritually-maturing family.

And he came and preached peace to you who were far off and peace to those who were near. For through him we both have access in one Spirit to the Father. So then you are no longer strangers and aliens, but you are fellow citizens with the saints and members of the household of God, built on the foundation of the apostles and prophets, Christ Jesus himself being the cornerstone, in whom the whole structure, being joined together, grows into a holy temple in the Lord. In Him you also are being built together into a dwelling place for God by the Spirit.

KIN

As God would have it, you and I aren't strangers . . . we are kin. Though this is true for us as part of His church, Jesus modeled the importance of funneling life down to closer relationships than that. The New Testament tells us that He spoke to large crowds, trained and sent seventy to spread the good news (Luke 10:1), shared life closely with twelve disciples (Matthew 10:2–4), and cultivated an exceptional depth with three among them (Mark 5:37; Matthew 17:1; Mark 14:33). That is what it takes to build relationships that can tell us (and transform us into) who we are in Christ.

Think of Peter. Among the twelve he was a shining star. The "rock" upon which the Church was built, his identity was firmly bestowed by Jesus Himself. Solidly walking the way of Christ, even Peter forgot who he was for a time. Just as Jesus foretold, before dawn's early light Peter's attachment to Jesus was broken and his identity quickly crumbled. He denied his connection to the Lord—not once but three times! Nonetheless, Jesus, being Jesus, returned to patiently repair and restore Peter's sense of who he was, reminding him out of love, "Feed my lambs. . . . Take care of my sheep. . . . Feed my sheep" (John 21:15–17).

Like Peter, we must gather around us a core group of people and learn to fiercely love and be loved by them. These are the ones who are committed to reminding us who God says we are. Just as with our families of origin, this small group family will require an abundance of grace in the form of the Four Amazing R's.

I used to run a marriage therapy program for couples in crisis. In my office hung a poster that captured one of my favorite quotes: "Remember as far as anybody knows, we are a nice, normal family." I think the same should hang in every church narthex too. Fairy tales don't automatically happen in church families any more than they do in our own families. Though God's household may feel safer thanks to His grace, life with the "relatives" in the extended church family can be just as messy as our own families of origin. Expect it. That being so, repairing and restoring are processes that we will need to practice together with special people we value. How does this happen? Where can you and I go to realize these healing forces?

It happens as we take time to connect with one another. Many church services are designed for two primary purposes: worship and teaching. Though we may catch a little connection from something our pastor said in church or from the warm smile of the chatty person we sat next to in the service, this setting is too big for meaningful grace-based attachments to form. The early church in Acts is noted to have congregated in the temple courts as well as in smaller groups that met in homes for meals and fellowship (Acts 2:42–47). Like them, regardless of the size of the congregation we attend, you and I need to engage regularly with a small group "family." We are built to be more than anonymous pew warmers. For grace-based attachment to form and our spiritual life to transform, these up-close, connected relationships are vital.

A robust life with God and others requires the reframing of an old paradigm: small group relationships are *family* relationships, and family instills identity. We need a community of close relationships—a group of fewer than twelve people—who authentically know us and allow themselves to be known by us. That means we live life together, we celebrate each other, and—when relationships get ruptured and our identity is rocked—the first thing we do is help one another repair and find restoration for our wounded identity.

Through his Word and in league with one another, you and I can affirm the treasure God sees within each of us. It's a practical and empowering gift we give one another as our connection grows. Because of God's plan for small groups, if and when my treasure somehow becomes tarnished, I know I can count on you and our group to help in my restoration process. In this way, you extend the gift of grace to me on God's behalf. We ebb and flow with one another, reciprocally dispensing God's grace to the degree that we are able. Instead of being abandoned to shame and dysfunction, our relationships help us to find our true selves again.

AGENTS OF GRACE

Apart from God and one another, we are incomplete—unable to receive, repair, or restore who we truly are. See why you matter here? Each of us needs people who *really* see and know who we are to remind us of who we are in Christ, especially during the times when we seem to forget. Apart from a close community, we cannot expect lasting spiritual transformation. You know the saying, "It takes a village"? Between us, we are called to show up with our offering of presence for one another— that includes our grace, our gifts, and our talents.

Despite what it may look like at a distance, a group of elite, highly trained ministry professionals is not solely responsible for our spiritual growth, or for repairing and restoring grace on the planet. Yes, church leaders have a role, but so do you and I! Pastors spend years training to preach, teach, prep and plan services, administer and manage church and staff, officiate at weddings and funerals—all as part of their calling. (Does this sound like a full plate to you?) Their focus is on leading and managing a group of people. Other than limited counseling duties, their primary role is facilitating these church functions—not working through the relational issues of church members. Though many pastors and staff long for the wholeness of their people, please note: creating and healing attachments and identity among congregants is outside the scope of what they are trained for in most seminaries and Bible colleges. Yes, some leaders have natural gifting in these areas, but they have a million other things to do.

The responsibility to help create and heal attachments and identity issues falls on each of us—not just the pros. It is an assignment you and I share: *we* are agents of grace. That means we need others close. To be a fully equipped, edified, and unified image of Jesus, I need what you have and vice versa. Ephesians 4:11–13 (NKJV) explains, "And He Himself gave some to be apostles, some prophets, some evangelists, and some pastors and teachers, for the equipping of the saints for the work of ministry, for the edifying of the body of Christ, till we all come to the unity of the faith and of the knowledge of the Son of God, to a perfect man, to the measure of the stature of the fullness of Christ."

From this passage it's unmistakable: God has provided gifted men and women to "equip" us. A look at the root of this Greek word, καταρτισμός, will help us better understand. Translated, it means much more than merely training another person for a specific task. It tells us that, as part of God's family, you and I are empowered (and, frankly, expected) to help repair, mend, make complete, restore one another. In other words, Paul is explaining to us that as God's family members we are responsible to help one another experience His grace. The "saints" are *us*, everyone in the body of Christ. That means, your everyday Christ-loving person is a minister, and that includes you and me! We are to work alongside church leaders in a daily, ongoing process of distributing God's grace in and between one another. By doing so, we help mend, repair, and restore one another in the name of Jesus. And Lord knows we need it!

God is clear that every one of us needs repairing and equipping. Every. Single. One. Please don't think I'm overlooking the importance of personal prayer, the study of Scripture, reflection, solitude, retreats, and the like. These things help you and me train for our spiritual growth. What I want to emphasize here is that if I were part of your small group, I need you to bring what you encounter on your own time with God back to the group—not to replace or neglect your practices of personal devotion. When we do this, you and I enjoy the rich marrow of relationship with God and one another. Again, we are given an opportunity to grow and know one another in Jesus. Each of us is built to equip, strengthen, and become a unifying force of faith—in love with Jesus and one another in these ways. Then, with eyes of grace, the fruit of the Spirit will flourish in our lives, and so will God's kingdom on Earth.

Based on what I've observed, grace profoundly changes lives within His family. I've seen countless numbers of men and women from all walks of life experience its power. One woman in particular comes to mind: Beth. Beth was a highly educated lawyer and, based on our counseling sessions, chronically angry and unhappy. Initially, she rejected the importance of grace. Then she joined a small group at her church and began to experience grace within the setting of God's family. Pretty quickly, everything about her began to change. Letting down the pretense of being a perfect Christian, she became more open and vulnerable. She recognized her need for grace-based attachment with others. Today, Beth will report that she is happier and more open than ever before. And she is committed to becoming a face of grace to those around her.

Beyond the example Beth has demonstrated, I've witnessed grace help people break free from years of addiction too. For that reason, many recovery programs camp on the fear of relapse. They know that for most of those in recovery, fear is what pushed them in the door to begin with—fear of dying, losing a marriage, getting fired, losing custody of their kids, etc. But grace changes that motive. It's like a magnet. Once an addict encounters grace-based loving relationships with God and others, these become like a tractor beam—pulling them toward personal, life-giving healing and recovery.

Some would tell you what they told me time after time: grace changed the spiritual atmosphere around them. Either these folks were actively participating as faces of grace in their environments, or they sought out those who could make them aware of God's presence in any given moment. As a way of life, they began to sense opportunities to join Him. They discovered the importance of being a face of grace.

It makes perfect sense, really. Within the family of God, grace is a catalyst for transformation in every area of life. A force to be reckoned with, it is God's vision for His special and favorite family members—and for those whom He still hopes to adopt. Grace-based relationships found here afford us what our families of origin could not, for whatever reason. It is the seedbed for encountering God's grace and presence. As these qualities take root in such a community, you and I will discover the love, joy, and peace to mend and repair what life has broken up until now. Within the family of God, we are meant to empower one another to grow, repair, and restore areas of life that would otherwise keep us from joyful attachment to one another.

If you think it doesn't matter whether you show up, you're wrong. Faith in Jesus was never meant to be a solo mission. He came for His *people*, not a general claim on the planet. He didn't walk through life without a small group family, so what's your rationale if you're not doing the same? Why else would He model for us a life full of relationships and a close community of others? Keep this front of mind: if you aren't intentional to pursue your days as an engaged, participating member of God's family, you will miss out on your spiritual growth. (Got questions and doubts? See the apostle Paul.) Your decision here has the potential either to build or to bust your identity—and your choice will ripple through eternity for us all. Show up for *us*!

INVITATION AND RELATIONSHIP

Remember: grace is both invitation *and* relationship. It is not informational dogma or head knowledge. What we learn in our small group *study* is a clear second to what we encounter in our small group *relationships*. When you and I invite others to join a small group "family," what we are actually saying is, "Come discover life with Jesus—let's share His presence and life."

God's transforming power will be unleashed in our lives as we regularly practice and experience the Four Amazing R's within our small group families. All the dynamics of our families of origin apply within our spiritual ones. In league with this close band of others, you and I will notice our rough edges begin to rub off. Then, walking more substantively in our real identity, we will experience the riches of ever-deepening relationships. And, before you and I may realize what is happening, the rich, real-time, grace-based encounters we share will turn our lives into beacons of God's glory. Progressively, grace will become part of who you and I are—and what we are known for. Our image will befit our Father—a magnetic people of shimmering joy. And therein lies your happy ending.

3 *The Focus of Small Groups*

The person who loves their dream of community will destroy community, but the person who loves those around them will create community.

—DIETRICH BONHOEFFER

Picture the face of your dearest friend. Now, think of the time you two had the most fun being together. What did you do? What did you talk about? How did it feel? Did you leave replenished? What made it so good?

Just like time alone with a good friend, spending time in God's presence is an essential part of getting to know and stay connected with Him. For me, this kind of time is vital to understanding who I am to God and helps define who He is to me. It is core to my identity. Alone with God, I experience a different dynamic than when I am with other people. In those undistracted moments, I listen, see, sense, and learn differently because I am one-on-one with Him. It is not better . . . just different. Still, if Jesus needed other people alongside him, so do I.

A few years ago, Greg Hawkins authored a book entitled *More: How to Move from Activity for God to Intimacy with God*. In it, he explained how community—life with close others—is "God's plan A" for our spiritual growth and transformation.

> From the beginning we were designed to do life together, with our hearts knitted together with the Father and with each other. We need others to tell us the truth, to hold us accountable, to encourage us, to laugh with us, to cry with us, to rejoice with us, and to simply experience life with us. In the beginning we had unity with God, and we had unity with each other. That's how it was supposed to be.[6]

If you lack that kind of community in your life, I hope to inspire you to seek it out because it is essential for a thriving spiritual life.

I have a few significant people who play a prominent role in God's Plan A for my life (my A-Team, as it were). Jim, Alan, Steve, and Trevor are each part of the close community I can depend on to remind me who I am, who God is, and who we are as a committed spiritual family.

Of course, my wife, Maritza, is also part of this inner circle. As a married couple in ministry together, the two of us have a divide-and-conquer approach that capitalizes on our individual strengths; Equipping Hearts for the Harvest, the ministry we founded together, simply couldn't exist without our partnership. But even more important than the ministry gifts she brings to our organization is how she reminds me of God's presence in the day-to-day. "You know He's holding your hand, right?" she'll say. Whether I'm teaching, writing, or creating, Maritza is a consistent and robust source of encouragement.

It would be easy for me to get lost in the mind-numbing detail that is required to keep things moving forward. Because Maritza is close, she can see and sense the times I need a reminder that God has a lot in store for us in our work. It's not manipulative or simply positive thinking. As part of my team, Maritza regularly provides my identity with a healthy booster shot—reminding me of how God sees me. Whether in the form of a spouse or a good friend, this is something we all need. These relationships hold a unique space in our hearts and minds. Hawkins refers to them as "deep friendships of unity" wherein we don't feel the need to compete or defend.[7] I just consider them my team.

So, who is on *your* A-Team roster? Picture those trusted companions who regularly point you to God in your own life. Recently, my friend Trevor provided a clear example of what I'm talking about. You see, I run the small group ministry for our church. I recruit, train, and mentor leaders, help them launch groups, and then support them any way I can. It is my heartbeat. First and foremost, more than curriculum or teaching, these small groups are organized around establishing the presence of God in the midst of the relationships represented. We start with a leader who feels passionate about something.

Our Games Group is a good example. Its leaders wanted to create a place where people could come to play games, eat, and get to know one another. A couple of families wanted to start it and open it up to the whole church. They are intentional to begin each meeting with prayer for the group and any needs the members may have. Then, they play. In my experience with *any* group, if you want to go the distance together, play is important. Whatever form it takes, play breaks down barriers and cultivates connection between people.

As part of that effort, our entire church was planning to get together to play volleyball, grill, and hang out—sponsored by our "Summer Games" small group. We talked up the party for weeks. Then, because I'd not been feeling well, at the last minute I had to forego the fun. I was so disappointed. I badly wanted to be there to support the leaders and connect with the broader community. My absence should have been the end of the story. But then my teammate, Trevor, called.

Trevor knew I'd be discouraged to miss being with everyone, so he called to tell me all about it. He said the event went exceptionally well and was a great time of fellowship. But when he finished recounting the festivities, Trevor wasn't finished encouraging me. He went on to tell me the story of Joe. Trevor had met him at another small group that week. Apparently, Joe went on and on about the blessing of family and community he and his small group were sharing. According to Trevor, Joe had never experienced this kind of community before. He was gushing with gratitude! More than just relaying details, Trevor knew, as my close friend, how that story would be extra important to me as the church's small group coordinator. That seemingly insignificant call deeply encouraged me—reminding me of my identity and significance and pointing to God's faithfulness.

FOCUS ON FIRST THINGS FIRST

By now I hope you have a clear picture of what I'm talking about. In our small groups, we need to focus on first things first—our number one priority is to experience God's presence together when we meet. Matthew 18:20 (NKJV) says, "For where two or three are gathered together in My name, I am there in the midst of them." Being part of a small group allows you and me to discover and experience God's presence in a different way than we can when we attempt to forge our faith life all alone. By organizing our time together around God's presence, we ensure that we are present with one another too. His presence can't help but radiate out of our lives on to those around us. These relationships are powerful.

Seeing one another through God's eyes of grace, a healthy group wants everyone onboard. First and foremost, that includes Jesus. Think of it this way: if Jesus were part of your small group, who would you want to lead? That simplifies things, wouldn't you say? He is among us—the primary sustainer of our gathering. Every. Time. He never misses a meeting. Yet in my years of ministry, more often than not, I've noticed that people quote the verse above, Matthew 18:20, as a de facto endorsement of their own agenda. The fact that Jesus would want to shepherd His sheep—to call and direct them according to what He is doing—tends to get overlooked.

The Lord's primary place in our midst empowers our presence with one another. If you and I miss this, we put the atmosphere and agenda of Jesus at stake in our own lives. We'd do well to be intentional. Has He been invited to the party? The heart of the question is this: do you and I orient our time around Him and the "things above" that surround His presence, as Scripture? (Be honest.) If not, we are treating Him like cheese dip—an appetizer before the main meal of whatever we are "really studying." Actually, what we need to set our sights on is maintaining a posture of loving presence with His presence in our midst. (Note: since we each play a part in ministering to one another, it's important to think about the group's intentions as well as your own.)

If we long to be formed into His image, our primary small group goal must be to encounter God's grace and presence. See why this is important? As you are changed, *so am I*. As I grow, *so can you*. We help one another. Invited, His presence will empower the time we have together—affording us vibrant life in the kingdom . . . now! Not only once we arrive in heaven. And there is a reciprocal nature to it. He delights to be among us as we delight in being together. Sharing experiences helps our identities mutually grow, repair, and restore.

As we discover life through eyes of grace, we encounter Jesus and see His heart and His presence among us. We begin to identify ourselves—His workmanship, a poetic work of art—as created *for* love and *to* love, designed to fulfill all He's prepared for us in advance (Ephesians 2:10). And once we begin to see ourselves that way, we will start to recognize the same in others. As a coordinated team, we help one another perceive a different angle on things—simultaneously, equally, and accurately.

THINGS ABOVE

How can small groups learn to cultivate and practice experiencing God's presence? It's not as hard and mystical as you may think. Colossians 3:1–4 (NKJV) gives us a clue:

> If then you were raised with Christ, seek those things which are above, where Christ is, sitting at the right hand of God. Set your mind on things above, not on things on the earth. For you died, and your life is hidden with Christ in God. When Christ who is our life appears, then you also will appear with Him in glory.

When we focus on "things above" when we get together, it's much easier for you and me to experience God's presence. Christ and our new life in Him are always in view. That's why grace-based small groups must always include activities that help us seek and become aware of Jesus' presence. In the next chapter, we will review some ways to help shift the focus to these important things.

By setting our minds on small group activities that help us experience, practice, and enjoy Jesus' presence, we become readily aware that He is with us. And the more that awareness grows, so do we. Grace is like that: it motivates change, whereas condemnation will shut it down. Opportunities for transformation abound as we share stories about our experiences with God's presence. You and I inspire each other that way! Grace and presence grow bonds between us. And as we've long since learned, what we love most affects our behavior. As a group, we begin to grow a life-changing group identity; we notice ourselves beginning to grow and change together.

Let me offer an example here. I have been part of a small group for the last five years. From the minute these dear ones come in the door, they reflect grace. There is just something about their faces—clearly, we are glad to be together. The hopeful expectation of our time is palpable. Usually we start by talking about things that we are grateful for or tell stories about how we have experienced God's presence since the last time we were together. All of this combines to multiply profound feelings of special and favorite—not just for me but for everyone.

I look forward to seeing my small group family! I mean, who wouldn't? Whenever we meet, things are noticeably brighter. These key people bring full color to my life; I feel markedly more connected, alive, loved, and loving because of them. My body feels warm, and my face beams just thinking about them. I liken it to replacing a 5-watt lightbulb with a 120-watt floodlight. We attend, we listen, we ponder together about the good things of God whenever we gather. Without fail, a sense of "Wow! I get to be part of this group of people?" takes over my thinking. It makes me want to share grace even more than I did the last time we met. And that is all the evidence I need: we are beacons of grace for one another, growing and changing all the time.

At its healthy best, our small group family is designed by God to be a place where we can join Him in things that . . .

- Build up
- Edify
- Comfort
- Nourish
- Produce maturity
- Provide healing
- Practically equip
- Help us grow into God's vision for our lives

Activating one another in these ways, you and I invite grace to get after God's good work—bringing change to our lives and the life of our small group community. We build bonds as we share stories of our individual experiences with God and enjoy life together. In combination, grace and presence have that effect. Our attachment grows in this setting, and so we are transformed. God knew what He was doing.

Be encouraged! This is possible for *any* group—that is, any group willing to focus on God's presence and things above. In the next chapter, we will delve into the ways to make this a reality for your small group, too, regardless of your format.

OUT OF FOCUS

Many of us have stories about small groups that haven't helped us become much more like Jesus. These groups may have delivered on helping with Scripture memory, Christian financial management, raising a godly family, etc., but overall the focus has been off. If our capacity to experience and extend grace-based attachment isn't an integral part of the format, the group is less likely to develop the relationships and strong biblical identity that lead to lasting transformation. That's not to say that groups like those mentioned aren't helpful, but they are informational, not relational, and information doesn't change you and me deep down.

Only grace-based relationships can bring enduring spiritual growth and transformation. If you're like me, you've been in a *looooooooot* of small groups over the years. Without fail, they all start out pretty well. You've got good reasons to join them. You may even "click" with some of the folks. But then, somehow, a few months or years down the road, things go south. You become bored, relationships sour, people want different material . . . who knows. The groups don't have staying power. Whatever the cause, internally you (and probably others in the group) are sent scrambling for an exit. What is that about anyway?

Small groups with staying power always lead with the Four Amazing R's that we discussed in the last chapter. Members are always about helping one another **Receive, Reflect, Repair,** and **Restore** their God-given identity as God's special and favorite. Content takes a backseat to relationship.

THE BIGFOOT OF SMALL GROUPS

As you participate in a small group, be aware of a few common myths that exist in the church world. It's important to know about them because otherwise they may sneak up on you and your people. Like Bigfoot, these myths are surrounded by enough "evidence" that they seem plausible, but when the truth comes out, each is a setup for disillusionment.

Myth #1: "Safe" Groups Exist

In the context of groups, grace sets up reasonable expectations, so here are a few things to let everyone know going in. If someone told you that you could find a "safe" group of people you trust and create a small group, they lied (okay, that may be a little severe, but they misguided you to think such a thing existed). No group will always be "safe" and "perfect." In fact, quite the opposite is true. Because groups are made of imperfect people (including ourselves), it's impossible to promise that they will always be completely 100 percent safe. Every group is "unsafe" and "imperfect." Things can *and will* go wrong. Guaranteed. Let everyone in your community know to expect it. But these "malfunctions" are a necessary part of actually experiencing—and growing in—authentic, grace-based community. And relational ruptures are not fatal. This is where repairing and restoring happen. Knowing this to be the case helps us bear—and be brave enough to face—the reality.

Perfection isn't realistic, and tolerance has a distinct odor. But authentic grace has a relaxed and delicious air about it—one that draws people in like warm chocolate chip cookies at an open house. Despite our failures, you and I desperately need to be seen for who we indeed are: God's special and favorite. Until we land in heaven, we all need to be seen, known, and reminded of it. Groups can unlock this part of our identity like no other.

Yes, sometimes it is possible to end up in a toxic group. But more often than not, what feels toxic is in reality just emotionally inconvenient, spiritually challenging, or otherwise uncomfortable. So you and I had best buck up and be there for one another—even when things feel awkward or dicey. Because most of us managed to miss the memo about seeing one another through God's eyes of grace, we also lost what Jesus meant in the Great Commandment—the part when He called us to love the Lord with all our heart, soul, mind, and strength, *and* to love our neighbor as ourselves.

Myth #2: Accountability Rules

Somewhere along the line, many good people have gotten the idea that accountability—not grace—rules in small groups. As such, they use the group setting as an opportunity to call others out on their sin (as if exposing another's shortcomings and checking back with them the next week will provide biblical accountability). When central to a group, an approach like this will often devolve into leveraging fear and shame to make one another behave. And if these become the basis for change, members will go into hiding, far from the light of grace and real biblical accountability.

Again, I'll put it bluntly: being overly focused on accountability is not appropriate or healthy for any grace-based small group community. Only the Holy Spirit is tasked with convicting a person of their sin, and even in that case, He never condemns. Instead, He seeks to kindly draw us kindly back to community through right, grace-centered relationship (Romans 2:4). Small groups that blast weaknesses are counterproductive and no less than destructive, both to a group and the individuals within them, especially if our objective is to plant seeds of grace-based bonds and cultivate their growth.

That is not to say that we wink at sin. God's grace and love are not blind. However, training ourselves to look at others with eyes of grace and love *first*, rather than leading with a sideways, judgmental glance, will enable us to see what others haven't yet seen for themselves. We will better represent the heart of Jesus to the one who missed the mark. Reminding someone of their redeemed identity is more likely to draw them in the same direction—and it leads our hearts a better way as well. This has proven true in several of my own relationships.

To be sure, accountability groups have their place. After all, there is such a thing as biblical accountability. It can happen in one of two ways: 1) I confess my fault to the group and invite their help, or 2) a group member recognizes that I'm behaving in a way that is inconsistent with my true identity and meets with me one-on-one to call me back to something better. In such a way, this person becomes an accountability partner by "speaking the truth in love" to help remind me who I am. Without a doubt, there are times when we all need reminding. Those who have held our history can speak light and love into these powerful moments.

Myth #3: Information = Discipleship

Learning information is not the same as discipleship. Jesus called us friends, not just followers. Nowhere in the Bible is discipleship ever separated from relationship. The Old Testament confirms how students of a rabbi were selected and expected to walk in close and constant relationship with their teacher. Ever wonder why? Information can't form the same loving attachments that grace does. Furthermore, when information becomes the basis for our attachment as a group, then we are destined to become like the Pharisees—focused more on the letter of the law than on the special and favorite ones in our midst.

Grace must be the foundation. Good information won't displace the fear that blocks spiritual growth and transformation. To become "little Christs," as C. S. Lewis called us, we need a full understanding of grace-based relationships. Let's take a closer look at what we are trying to accomplish and whether we are setting our groups up for success.

THE OLD PRESCRIPTION

Ever had your eyes checked? The optometrist sits you in a chair, runs you through a battery of tests. Ultimately, you watch as the lenses of a phoropter flip by until the right prescription is determined to return your vision to 20/20. The right lenses will change your world! That being said, I think it would be wise for anyone leading (or planning to lead) a small group to get a vision check. Otherwise, if you and I are not seeing clearly, we may miss out on essential small group dynamics that lead to transformation. A couple of small group models in need of new lenses include what I call Nearsighted Traditional Bible Studies and Farsighted Sharing Groups.

Nearsighted Traditional Bible Studies. Traditional Bible studies are usually led by one person who shares a passage of Scripture (or curriculum), teaches about it, and offers their insights. I call this "nearsighted" because the focus is what's up in front; the group bonds over the leader's ability to teach or expound on Scripture. Subsequent discussion revolves around insights gained from the teaching or personal application of the Scripture and its relevance to the lives of those in the group.

Certainly, I'm not suggesting that Bible study is inherently wrong, but I *am* suggesting that this kind of group is limited by the following factors:

- One person's gifts become the focus of the group.
- The group bonds around the teacher and his or her gifts and the communication of information.
- Participants often remain in a position of "passive learner."
- There is a lack of mutuality in sharing gifts and grace.
- These groups can go south very quickly if the leader is narcissistic, codependent, or interested in pursuing a personal platform for ministry.

Imagine if there was a way for groups to study Scripture together so that everyone could share what they experienced while reflecting on a passage of Scripture along with Jesus. We will explore that possibility further in the next chapter.

Farsighted Sharing Groups. Sharing groups are "farsighted" because they, too, miss the big picture right in front of them. Jesus' presence is bigger than their pain, yet they primarily orient around feelings, problems, trauma, or opinions. My forty years of experience conducting small groups have demonstrated the limitations of sharing groups:

- These groups sometimes revolve around people who are either doing exceedingly well or the opposite.
- In most cases, they become overly focused on the person or people in the most pain or biggest crisis at the time the group meets. Thus, the group becomes problem centered and not grace or Presence centered.
- Either of the scenarios above is a setup for codependent rescues and especially codependent prayers.
- Because problems and pain become the focus of the group, members don't mature in grace.
- Likewise, healthy attachments and grace-based identity change don't occur because of the focus on problems and pain.
- Group members in the most pain set the agenda for the rest of the group.

What if there was a way to pray for real needs after experiencing and sharing God's presence and grace? There is, and we will discover more about that shortly.

There is a place for both traditional Bible study groups and sharing groups as long as objectives are clear. With biblical illiteracy at a crisis level in our country, there is an obvious need for Bible study! Yet as important as attending a Bible class may be, it is not the same thing as attending a small group. At a typical Bible study, someone (or a video curriculum) teaches, and then people discuss or share. It's a classroom setting, see? Support groups like AA are also important as people work through addiction. But again, for spiritual maturity and transformation, sharing groups are no replacement for participating in a grace-based small group. It's time to reassess these standard approaches. Their prescription as a cure for common religion has most definitely expired! The focus of grace-based small groups is simply different.

CLEAR VISION FOR SMALL GROUP DYNAMICS

When I look at various models of small group community these days, many seem to be a little fuzzy about what a discipleship group looks like. We are so used to seeing a limited image of what it *could* be that perhaps we haven't considered that our collective vision may be impaired. As a result, because our vision is impaired, our goals and expectations are too. If the goal of small groups is to create disciples, a common vision is vital.

Only a small group that is laser focused on an entirely relational process of sharing grace—being special and favorite to one another—will develop the kind of secure attachments with God and other people required for spiritual life-change. In such settings, our Father's presence is central and everyone's input is equal. Our time is focused on small group activities that practice His presence. This simple dynamic holds the hope of producing healthy small groups whose members have internalized both a biblical individual and biblical group identity that can lead to their transformation into Christlikeness. A new way of being is actualized. God's kingdom is brought to Earth through His presence in our small group relationships.

4 Superheroes and Small Group Activities

Since, then, you have been raised with Christ, set your hearts on things above, where Christ is, seated at the right hand of God. Set your minds on things above, not on earthly things. For you died, and your life is now hidden with Christ in God. When Christ, who is your life, appears, then you also will appear with him in glory.

—COLOSSIANS 3:1–4

Sometime before his death in 2018, comic book legend Stan Lee was invited to contribute an essay for a book entitled *What Is a Superhero?* For his part, the man who made many modern superheroes a household name explained that a "superhero is a person who does heroic deeds and has the ability to do them in a way that a normal person couldn't. So in order to be a superhero, you need a power that is more exceptional than any power a normal human being could possess, and you need to use that power to accomplish good deeds."[8]

By that definition—together and through the power of the Holy Spirit—you and I are in a league of superheroes. We *all* are. The reality is, our superpowers are activated in grace-based relationships with God and others.

When I was a kid, my favorite superhero was Superman. I got the costume and all the accessories to go with it. Despite my lack of actual superpowers, I'd spend hours in make-believe battles, vanquishing bad guys. However, I knew when the costume came off, so did my imaginary superpowers. You'll be glad to know that I eventually outgrew my childish obsession, and, while it was a lot of fun, I've turned my attention to helping people develop the real-life superpower of grace-based attachment. The basics are the basis for a superhuman transformation of the galaxy. The kind Jesus has in mind.

CAN WE AGREE: THE CHURCH UNIVERSE NEEDS SOME HEROES?

Despite sincere hearts and valiant efforts, church membership and weekend services haven't provided what is needed for soul transformation. After all, there are limits—just so much can happen one morning a week. That's because good teaching and worship can only take people so far on their spiritual journeys. To think otherwise is a setup for disillusionment.

The way we "do church" also encourages the very Western idea that our spiritual life is all about us—our needs, our fulfillment, and even our entertainment. Showing up to listen once a week makes us feel good. What's really happening? Our rugged individualism is crippling the power of our faith in Jesus, leaving many pew squatters spiritually immature and disconnected from the power of community. (If Superman had never known the nurture of Ma and Pa Kent, would he have grown to use his powers for good?)

A lone-ranger mind-set is our kryptonite. It weakens our God-given strengths in one of two ways:

1. It tricks us into believing we have more power/knowledge/ gifting than others in our community, leaving us to feel we don't need others because of our superior gifts and abilities.

2. It causes us to buy into the idea that others in our group are "stronger" than we are, and therefore we defer to them.

Who can save us?!

BE HAPPY

Did you know the United Nations releases a World Happiness Report each year? Officially, the report "is a landmark survey of the state of global happiness that ranks 156 countries by how happy their citizens perceive themselves to be."[9]

When you consider the freedom and prosperity we enjoy in the United States, wouldn't you think we'd top the happy pile? Sadly, we aren't even in the top ten. From year to year, the cultures where people enjoy being together (sharing social support, sharing the bounty of their gardens, growing up and old together) are markedly more fulfilled. Companioning one another in all aspects of life, the world's most fulfilled individuals demonstrate a special-and-favorite lifestyle—in such a way that it has tipped the global scale.

Oh, what the Christian church could learn from these happy places.

No one, not even a group leader, has a corner on superpowers. We all have the opportunity to bring a part of the character of Jesus to life and let it flow through our unique gifting. Though sometimes we may prefer to fly under the radar, we must engage with Jesus and one another.

Failure to engage with Jesus and one another comes at a high cost. Nothing can replace the bond of grace-based relationships—not pew sitting, not social media, not biblical scholarship, not even doing good deeds. Heart, soul, and mind, we must have face-to-face relationships with others to be well. The United Kingdom has taken notice. According to research they did in conjunction with the Red Cross, loneliness is worse for you than smoking fifteen cigarettes a day. The findings motivated the country to establish a Ministry of Loneliness in 2018.[10]

If you and I want to build a thriving small group, we need to think of ourselves like directors for our league of superheroes (don't be uncomfortable: all superheroes have one). Flowing naturally from a base of grace, a good director's leadership keeps the mission in focus and on task. Part of his or her responsibility involves creating a framework that strategically calls up the strength of each team member at just the right time. Doing so allows everyone to grow together. Recognizing individual needs along the way creates an environment within the league that encourages care and collaboration for the greater good.

PUTTING ON "THINGS ABOVE"

The *Beyond Becoming* activities outlined in part 2 provide a framework to help people engage with God and each other. Within the context of a small group, they help us train for what Colossians 3:12–15 (esv) talks about: "Put on then, as God's chosen ones, holy and beloved, compassionate hearts, kindness, humility, meekness, and patience, bearing with one another and, if one has a complaint against another, forgiving each other; as the Lord has forgiven you, so you also must forgive. And above all these put on love, which binds everything together in perfect harmony. And let the peace of Christ rule in your hearts, to which indeed you were called in one body. And be thankful." I encourage you to experiment with the activities and find the ones you are most comfortable using. Because these are in the DNA of true fellowship, it's important to weave them into various aspects of your meetings. As you anchor yourself and your group in God's presence and the presence of one another, each activity has the potential to strengthen your grace-based attachments. *Beyond Becoming* activities include the following:

1. **Growing Gratitude**—Sharing experiences and moments that have inspired gratitude and appreciation in our daily lives.

2. **Jesus Moments and Jesus Stories**—Sharing moments when we have experienced Jesus' very real presence.

3. **Quieting to Connect**—Quieting and resting our thoughts and emotions by slowing down, breathing, relaxing, and connecting with Jesus.

4. **Joining with Jesus**—Interceding for others by first asking Jesus how He is praying for others in the group.

5. **Scripture Reflection**—Facilitating Group Scripture Reflection by paying attention to the Holy Spirit's leading and then sharing our insights.

6. **Conversation with Jesus**—Interacting with Jesus and sharing stories about that interaction. (This activity combines some of the others.)

7. **Finding Shoes That Fit**—Customizing *Beyond Becoming* activities to fit your group.

Taking time with each activity allows us to experience deep expressions of grace together. These connections grow more deeply as we keep God in the center of them. Following His lead, you and I will discover more about our individual identity. Simultaneously, our group identity will become more important as we help one another define who we are and how we can grow together. With efforts and hearts combined, you and I will find ourselves moving forward toward spiritual maturity.

LEVERAGING OUR INFLUENCE

Building prayerfully (and with grace) around the strengths and needs of our members, it is time to consider a couple of tried-and-true methods to leverage our efforts. Guaranteed, the purposeful decisions we make will pay off in time, in the form of spiritual enrichment and emotional currency for all involved. Adding them to your repertoire will help build bonds as well as a sense of purpose among discipleship group members.

Meals

Maritza often reminds me, Western Christians are, by and large, "relationally anorexic." Therefore, meals—along with the other activities we will cover—are means of bulking up our connections with others to make up for the deprivation that is all too common among us. From the beginning of life, attachment is our greatest need. It is the way we form bonds and learn who we are in the world. Even when fully grown, you and I continue to discern our worth from those who feed, care for, and gather around the table with us. That's why sharing meals echoes a sense of this bonding. Back in Old Testament days, sharing a meal set a tone of grace. Today, eating together "is an almost universal medium for expressing fellowship; it embodies values of hospitality, duty, gratitude, sacrifice, and compassion. The shared meal is an opportunity not only to eat but also to talk, to create and strengthen bonds of attachment and friendship, to teach and learn."[11] Eating together is a huge opportunity for grace-based attachment.

Play

Play is the joyful thread that ties together our days—especially play that involves others with whom we are close. Whatever the topic or reason a group may gather around, play has a powerful way of uncovering our identity. It also develops bonds between us. In his book *Play: How It*

Shapes the Brain, Opens the Imagination, and Invigorates the Soul, author Stuart Brown writes, "Of all animal species, humans are the biggest players of all. We are built to play and built through play. When we play, we are engaged in the purest expression of our humanity, the truest expression of our individuality. Is it any wonder that often the times we feel most alive, those that make up our best memories, are moments of play? . . . The ability to play is critical not only to be happy but also to sustaining social relationships and being a creative, innovative person."[12]

It is a counterbalance to hardship, a positive to negatives. Even if just in the moment, play can help heal what hurts us as we actively engage with one another and realize that we are not alone. Play teaches us—it is one of the most effective teaching tools around. Play inherently injects life into our community in novel and unexpected ways. It actively engages us with each other, enabling us to make the kind of meaningful connections that help us learn and grow in new spiritual, physical, social, emotional, and creative ways. Because we are playing, most of the time you and I hardly even notice these important "side effects."

Several years ago, I led a group that scheduled a time to play together once each quarter. One of those times we planned a cookout at a lake. We floated around in inner tubes, had water fights, and relaxed together for most of the day. At one point one lady looked at me and said, "I really love this! This kind of time with everyone is as important to me as our regular meetings." Her simple statement has stuck with me over the years. She was right. Our playtimes felt like a different kind of important than our usual small group meetings. Playing together generates powerful, lasting relationships.

Both meals and play get us out of our heads and comfort zones, allowing us to lose track of ourselves and enjoy informal ways of connecting. Here, the bonds we grow help us realize how much we need grace and increase our desire to give it to others. By design, these undirected, joyful, engaging, and social spaces all provide stuff you can't get in a classroom. By occasionally adding these elements to a small group schedule, we provide tremendous (and covert) opportunities to amplify grace-based attachment.

No matter which way you and I choose to organize our group time, being present in God's presence helps us to make Him the center, before tactically inviting Him into our midst through *Beyond Becoming* activities.

CREATIVITY AND THE SUPERPOWER OF LEADERSHIP

We've made it pretty clear: it's not about *us*. Our leadership should neither distract from the group nor cause us to shrink back from our true identity—and all the good things that come with it. Part of the beauty of grace-based community is that it unmasks *all of us*—displaying the gifts, talents, calling, and superhuman strength in our hearts.

Combined with God's grace, these forces creatively empower the uniqueness of our dynamic leadership style. That is why every time I help launch a group, I ask leaders to consider more than their willingness to lead a small group fellowship. I ask them *why they want to lead their group and* encourage them to share the vision of the change they feel called to lead by asking questions like these:

- What do you love doing and want to share with others?
- What dynamics of discipleship would you like to see as a result of gathering this way?
- Is there a theme you can develop from your answers above?
- If you follow God's design for your group, what will your time together look like?
- From that design, how will the group impact your group members' lives?

Unleashing our creative energy in a small group allows us to set goals that authentically reflect God's design. For example, one couple

I work with is passionate about financial responsibility and lead Dave Ramsey's Financial Peace University. Moved to serve church members in our area, another guy organized a community service group. A young family whose son is really into sports translated their love of play into a small group format, and every summer they invite our entire church to their Summer Games. Our whole church is better for these diverse and sincere demonstrations of leadership.

Of course, for each small group the logistics are different, but the focus is *always* fellowship. That is because fellowship, more than anything else, is a gateway to spiritual growth. Get the idea? Here are some interests and themes that small groups may launch from:

- Sports (e.g., hiking, running, basketball, skiing, tennis)
- Sermon discussion groups
- Strengthening marriage
- Raising healthy kids
- Church and community service
- Creativity (e.g., art, photography, fiber art, writing)
- Business mastermind
- Worship
- Prayer

When training small group leaders, I require them to learn and practice each of the *Beyond Becoming* activities in order to determine those that best suit them and their group. What seems like a natural fit? This is important because I suggest that at least one or two of the activities be integrated into each gathering. Sometimes a small group's theme will make the choices obvious. For instance, the Financial Peace University group mentioned earlier follows a video curriculum and workbook. It would make sense that they incorporate the less time-consuming practices on the list, like the Growing Gratitude and Quieting to Connect activities. Another example is a Sermon Discussion group. Since the content is dictated by the pastor's message, perhaps a relevant Scripture Reflection activity and the sharing of Jesus Moments and Jesus Stories would be a good combination. Whichever you choose, keep in mind that the goal is to create opportunities for your fellowship community to build lasting, relational connections.

As group leaders, these activities are bound to influence our spiritual formation as well as our group's. Once we become comfortable with these practices in our own spiritual lives, we will discover enormous freedom to explore what sparks the group each time we meet. Follow wherever the Spirit leads. Remember:

- These concepts are intended for your spiritual transformation as well as that of each of your group members.
- The purpose of a small group is to grow grace in our lives. These activities build grace-based attachments.
- These general structures should be tailored to your group of superheroes.
- Teachability is measured by humility. Teachability is mirrored. Practice what you teach.
- In the following chapters, we are going to explore each of the *Beyond Becoming* activities in greater depth.

Discipleship is Christlike-character building. As you and I grow closer to God and others, it reveals our true identity. Knowing with certainty that God sees you and me as super-special and super-favorite, the skills we adopt between here and the final pages of this book will show us how to live as champions in God's universe of grace-based relationship.

PART 2

ACTIVITIES FOR
GRACE-BASED SMALL GROUPS

5 *Growing Gratitude: Cultivating a Grateful Heart*

When it comes to life, the critical thing is whether you take things for granted or take them with gratitude.

—G. K. CHESTERTON

My days are pretty unpredictable. In addition to my personal life, much of what I do is so relationally oriented that there's a certain X factor to what will happen or be needed. Honestly, there is no such thing as a "normal" day for me much beyond how each begins: coffee. Not black but swirling with coconut milk creamer (*Inhale. Ahhh.*) Invariably, I roll out of bed while it's still dark, make my way to the kitchen, and pour a freshly brewed cup. From there I shuffle to the refrigerator to stir in the creamer and draw a long, slow breath. I'm up. Savoring its aroma and the eye-opening gift that it is, I anticipate the robust, comforting flavor in my cup. What makes it even richer is what it reminds me of: my quiet time with Jesus.

That is what comes next.

Walking into the living room, I plop down on the couch holding my mug. I prop up my feet next to my Bible, journal, and a choice book selection, not too far from the view of our big sliding glass door. Coffee and quiet time combine for an atmosphere of wakeful presence. I welcome the Lord into the day ahead. Every day, I look forward to this joyful start. Stirring an awareness of God's presence, a simple cup of coconut coffee reminds me I'm grateful for so much more.

Not for a minute am I suggesting you run out and buy coffee or coconut milk creamer. What I *am* suggesting is that gratitude is not a heady, heavy, or hard activity to incorporate. A gratitude practice is holy and essential work. It only requires a little self-discipline to get started. Is coffee a spiritual practice then? Why yes, for me I'd say that it is, albeit perhaps nontraditional. Coffee clears the morning fog to inspire my first thoughts of God. From the start, it primes me to turn my awareness to the Giver. Paying attention, I am gratefully reminded to practice His presence.

Growing Gratitude began as a challenge from my friend Alan. "Just start your quiet time by thinking of one thing that you're grateful for," he urged. Brilliant! Over time, it changed me—my days seemed to unfold differently. Paying attention to what sparks appreciation in my heart throughout the day—being on "gratitude watch"—sets a hopeful expectation for virtually everything I experience.

WHAT THE WORD SAYS ABOUT GRATITUDE

The Bible gives us good reason to incorporate the practice of gratitude into our days. In the Old Testament, the word *tôdâh* (pronounced to-daw) translates to mean "thanksgiving or gratitude." Used properly it implies the extending of a hand in praise or adoration. It can be a part of worship, a confession, a sacrifice of praise, or an offering of thanksgiving.

According to Scripture, gratitude is important for the following reasons:

- It is how we come into God's Presence (Psalm 100:4).
- It is voluntary (Leviticus 22:18–19).
- God knows it will lead us to life (Psalm 69:30–32).

- God desires our gratitude more than any duty, obligation, or legalism we manufacture (Psalm 50:7–15).

There is a strong, unavoidable connection between grace and thanksgiving. The New Testament captures gratitude with the Greek word *eucharistia* (pronounced yoo-khar-is-tee'-ah). In Paul's writings, he refers to the expression of gratitude as thanks to God, grateful speech or conversation.[13] *Eucharistia* is derived from the Greek word *charis*, which literally means grace, and rightly implies a position of favor, a kindness or rescue freely given. You see, thanksgiving is a direct response to God's incredible grace (2 Corinthians 4:15). Notice the similarity to the language used for Holy Communion, i.e., the Eucharist)? All of this raises the question, if we are truly connected to God, is there such a thing as experiencing grace *without* thanksgiving? Clearly, gratitude is an active response to God's grace in all its forms. Along with other expressions of thanks, it reflects

- our new identity in Christ (Ephesians 2:1–10)
- the mind-set and attitude with which we serve (Hebrews 12:28)
- a key part of prayer (Colossians 4:2)
- a connection with God's peace—and who doesn't want more peace? (Colossians 3:15)
- what's happening in heaven, inviting us to join in (Revelation 4:8–11; 7:11–12)
- the bad things that happen to our minds when we are not grateful (Romans 1:21–23)

DEEP CALLS TO DEEP

When you and I share stories of appreciation, it "primes the pump"—and once it becomes a habit to tell others about the good things we notice, more good things will flow. Slowing down and paying attention to what brings us joy allows us to reflect more deeply. If we do so long enough, our bodies will begin to echo the feelings and emotions that came with it. (Remember my coffee and coconut creamer? It's as simple as pausing to take a deep breath of goodness).

Learning to grow gratitude helps people express aspects of themselves that may otherwise go unnoticed—by them or by others. This includes both physical feelings and emotions. Sadly, there are a lot of sincere followers of Jesus out there who have never felt the deep-reaching feeling or bodily sensation of gratitude. It's like eating dry cake with no icing at a party. We do it to be polite. Some dutiful, hardworking people of faith have little or no frosting in either category—but it's never too late to add some to the mix. When we gratefully remember a thing and reflect on it long enough, physical and emotional feelings will recreate themselves in our bodies. In effect, when you and I remember and express gratitude in this way, we are writing a personal psalm.

DAVID: OUR MODEL

Scripturally speaking, throughout the Psalms David modeled how to grow gratitude. Here are some examples of verses where he expressed both emotions and the bodily sensations that accompanied them. As you read them, imagine his feelings and what he may have physically experienced in his body according to how he described them. Make them yours.

- Psalm 18:4–5 "The cords of death entangled me; the torrents of destruction overwhelmed me. The cords of the grave coiled around me; the snares of death confronted me."
- Psalm 4:8 "In peace I will lie down and sleep, for you alone, LORD, make me dwell in safety."
- Psalm 6:6–7 "I am worn out from my groaning. All night long I flood my bed with weeping and drench my couch

with tears. My eyes grow weak with sorrow; they fail because of all my foes."

- Psalm 23 (entire chapter)
- Psalm 42:7–8 "Deep calls to deep in the roar of your waterfalls; all your waves and breakers have swept over me. By day the LORD directs his love, at night his song is with me—a prayer to the God of my life."
- Psalm 84:2 "My soul yearns, even faints, for the courts of the LORD: my heart and my flesh cry out for the living God."
- Psalm 126:2 "Our mouths were filled with laughter, our tongues with songs of joy. Then it was said among the nations, 'The LORD has done great things for them.'"
- Psalm 131:1–2 "My heart is not proud, LORD, my eyes are not haughty; I do not concern myself with great matters or things too wonderful for me. But I have calmed and quieted myself, I am like a weaned child with its mother; like a weaned child I am content."
- Psalm 139 (entire chapter)

GROWING GRATITUDE MATTERS

Our gratitude stories matter because they encourage us and those listening. Gratitude amplifies gratitude. Our feelings inspire and resonate with those around us, inspiring others to start noticing the same kinds of things in their own lives. Can you imagine what our churches would be like if everyone began Growing Gratitude? Help welcome this exciting spiritual dynamic into your community and watch the atmosphere shift.

Want another important reason to practice gratitude? In our years helping to train missionaries around the world, Maritza and I have learned that the number one reason they leave the mission field is relational burnout. Bottom line: they can't get along with others. At a certain point, it exhausts them. The same can be said for married couples, parents, employees, children—pretty much everyone ever. Sometimes relationships make us want to quit. There are a lot of reasons for what this is about and the ways that it happens, but one thing is sure: conflict is a normal and inevitable part of life. We would be wise to help equip one another to deal with it.

No matter how nice people are when you and I first meet them, eventually we will have disagreements. But we don't need to run from our differences. Whatever side we find ourselves on, you and I can consider any conflict an opportunity for Growing Gratitude. If we train our hearts to look at people with appreciation in calmer times (and go so far as to develop a list of things we are grateful for about them), it will be harder to forget their good parts later—even in a heated argument. A list of things you appreciate about others strengthens your capacity to stay engaged when the going gets rough. The result? An opportunity for your grace-based relationship to grow!

Activity #1: Growing Gratitude—Cultivating a Thankful Heart

When we tell stories about ourselves, you and I get to know one another. Learning what inspires gratitude has that effect. It's simple really. Throughout each day, look for Gratitude Moments. Simply, pay attention to the people and things that make you feel grateful—those that inspire appreciation or worship. As you do, write them down. Each time you meet with your group, select one shareable moment that stands out. The following framework demonstrates how easy it is to share and grow in gratitude with others, in order to "shift the atmosphere" of our days.[14] Between meetings, use the space below to record your reflections each day.

For a downloadable version of this worksheet, visit
www.equippinghearts.com

Briefly describe what happened in your Gratitude Moment.

Take a minute to consider what it felt like at the time. Remember David's example as you list the emotional and physical responses that you experienced in your moment of thanksgiving. List them here.

What did you do when you felt gratitude? (Did you thank God, thank another, cheer?)

How would you like to thank God right now?

(Note for group leaders: Next time you meet, break your small group into groups of three and ask them to select one of their Gratitude Moments from the week to briefly share. Give them three minutes each. Due to time constraints, remind them to follow the guidelines below and not to provide backstory unless it is absolutely necessary.)

Sharing stories works best when we remember to do the following:

- Keep the focus on gratitude and the thanksgiving it inspires. Because each person will just have three minutes to tell their story, remember not to provide backstory if possible.
- Allow your authentic feelings of gratitude to show on your face and in your tone of voice.
- Make eye contact (as much as feels comfortable). People connect best when looking one another in the eye.
- Tell a story that you won't later feel bad about having shared.

(Note to group leaders: Since this activity promotes bonding by sharing grace, split members into groups of three. Give each person three minutes to share one Gratitude Moment from the week. Brief stories intentionally keep the focus on the worship and appreciation inspired by the Gratitude Moments.)

Growing Gratitude: Amanda's Story

When I woke up that winter morning, it was a typical overcast midwestern day. I was well rested and ready to take it on. I made my usual stop for coffee and continued on my way to work. Then, for whatever reason, I started getting irritated. Soon I found myself flat-out angry. I started spiraling down into all the things I hate. "I hate this traffic, I hate my job, I'm sick of no one in my family being there for me. I'm so angry that I could just crash this stupid car! That would feel so good right now! Maybe that will make these feelings go away." (I honestly thought that was a viable solution?!) The further along on my commute I rolled, the more furious I became. It consumed me to the point that my body was shaking, my jaw felt like a vise, and my foot weighed heavily on the pedals. *Gas, brake, gas*, I stomped. I could tell I wasn't okay.

It was ironic really. At the time I was in a study group that was working on cultivating gratitude in our lives—even when things were bad. We'd been meeting for a few months when this happened, and I had already found what I was learning to be ridiculously practical. I'd been noticing how reflecting on things I was thankful for had been subtly effective. Things in my life were changing for the better. But I must admit since beginning the practice of Growing Gratitude, I hadn't encountered such a surge of negative emotion. Suddenly it occurred to me: *This is a good lab test.* Quickly, I tried to think of something I appreciated to keep me off the concrete barricade on my right. Nothing came immediately to mind. *This is silly. I'm sure there is* something.

Gripping the steering wheel tightly, I realized, *Okay, I have a nice car. I appreciate that I have a car.* Immediately, some of the angry weight lifted off of my chest. *Okay, I have a great friend group. I am grateful for my friends.* Again, the weight continued to lift, and feeling gratitude became easier. Before long I was smiling and laughing. (I'll be honest, I felt a little crazy.) I came to my senses and realized the anger that almost made me want to wreck my car was completely gone.

Not only that, but I suddenly recognized feelings of joy surrounding all the things I appreciated in my life. In real time, it only took a couple of moments. The effectiveness of that exercise took me completely by surprise. Thinking about my study group, I was excited to share the dramatic change that had occurred in me. The enemy had tried to derail me with anger, but Jesus had protected me with a simple gratitude practice that led me back to His joy.

6 *Jesus Moments and Jesus Stories*

The time of business does not differ with me from the time of prayer; and in the noise and clatter of my kitchen, while several persons are at the same time calling for different things, I possess God in as great a tranquility as if I were upon my knees at the blessed sacrament.

—BROTHER LAWRENCE

If you are at all like me, you want to develop an increasing awareness of Jesus' presence in all areas of life. Though we may have particular places we go or things we do that remind us of Him, many of us lack a conscious ongoing awareness of Jesus' interactive presence in our everyday dealings. For those who stare blankly when reading these words, I have good news: it's not hard or for the lucky few. Jesus Stories are like Gratitude Moments—the more we look for those moments, the more we will find them.

This is Immanuel's way—*God with us!* By simply paying attention, and reflecting more deeply on our own experiences, we will begin to recognize His presence with us throughout the day. It is similar to the

Growing Gratitude activity but different. Jesus Stories are way more powerful because with Jesus Stories you and I are looking for times when we have experienced direct interaction with Him. Getting in the habit of noticing His presence builds our capacity to connect with God. This goes way beyond mentally assenting to the scriptural idea that He is always with us. Very specifically, the closeness of a Jesus Moment—the source of our Jesus Story—identifies itself when His presence affects us in emotional and physical ways. Remembering them brings us hope, peace, and joy. Now, let me tell you a story . . .

Imagine again the scene from the last chapter: it's early morning and I'm sitting in my living room holding my steaming mug of coconut coffee. Lately, I've been making my way through 1 and 2 Peter, and everything I read seems to guide me to the topic of God's grace. This day in particular, I feel like the Lord is sitting beside me, eagerly pointing me to it. *"See! It's* here . . . *and* here . . . *and* here!" He directs. Together, we are smiling as He unpacks these scriptures in ways He knows I need to hear. We laugh at how clear He has made it. Feeling light and love, I can tell I am the center of His attention—and He is the center of mine! As my quiet time comes to a close, already I can't wait to wake up and be with God again tomorrow.

That is presence. That is my Jesus Story.

WHY SHARE JESUS STORIES?

Aside from the fun of communicating your excitement, there are a lot of good reasons for sharing Jesus Stories in your group. Jesus Stories

- help focus the group on Jesus' presence, goodness, and love *first*. Sharing Jesus Stories will change the atmosphere for everything that follows.
- provide a good place to *begin* praying for someone else.
- build faith and hopeful expectancy, both for the person sharing and those listening.

- help us discover a new "normal" that is characterized by God's presence.
- make it much easier to be led by the Spirit (actively looking for God's presence has that effect).
- present us with simple opportunities to share our faith (no one can argue with your experience).
- are testimonies to share with others.

Whenever you and I reflect on our Jesus Moments, they spring back to life. Spiritual dynamics are revived—encouraging our hearts and the hearts of all who hear about our experience. As they say, "Jesus is in the building"; who knows what will happen next? (Whatever it is, I'm sure you'll hear a story about it.)

Activity #2: Jesus Moments and Jesus Stories

Jesus *Moments* remind us of God's presence—they get us in the habit of paying attention to His presence at any given moment. Jesus *Stories* build on a Jesus Moment with more detail. They retell the details of specific exchanges we've had with Him (often involving insights the Lord has given, feelings, or physical reactions—like peace or a smile). For this *Beyond Becoming* activity, you will be looking each day for moments when you experience Jesus' presence. Use the worksheet below to track them and prepare your story.

Briefly describe what happened in each of your Jesus Moments.

Take a minute to consider what it felt like at the time. Remember to include the emotional and physical responses that you experienced in your Jesus Moments. List them here.

Briefly describe what you did when you realized that Jesus was with you. (Did you thank Him, weep, hug Him, tell someone, etc.?)

How would you like to thank God right now for the moment you shared with Jesus?

(Note to group leaders: You will notice that the directions for sharing Jesus Moments and Jesus Stories are similar to those in the last chapter for the Growing Gratitude activity next time you meet, break members into groups of three and instruct group members to briefly share one of your Jesus Stories with one another. Encourage them to notice how it feels to share their story as well as how it feels to listen to other group members' stories.)

For a downloadable version of this worksheet, visit
www.equippinghearts.com

Keep in mind, sharing stories works best when you remember to do the following:

- Keep the focus on Jesus' presence and how it inspires you to pray.
- Avoid giving too much detail. Because each person will just have three minutes to tell their story, only provide backstory if it is necessary.
- Allow your authentic feelings to show on your face and in your tone of voice.
- Make eye contact (as much as feels comfortable). People connect best when looking at one another in the eye.
- Tell a story that you won't feel bad later about having shared.

Jesus Moments and Jesus Stories: Drew's Story

We were a family of five drivers and one car. Getting everyone to work and school (let alone teenage activities and social obligations) was a challenge. When a dear friend offered to give us a small truck that he wanted to get rid of, my wife and I gratefully and eagerly accepted it. Beth and I determined it would be the car I'd use for work. It was nothing fancy, to say the least, but I didn't mind. I used my phone for music and rolled the windows down for "air conditioning." I was thankful to have four wheels and a roof.

Needless to say, I was also glad to have a trusted mechanic that had worked on our other car for years. You could tell by looking at our newly acquired vehicle that his help would come in handy. Even though his garage was an hour north of us, he was fair and dependable—it was worth the trip. One day, I started up I-85 for what was a scheduled, routine repair.

As I merged onto the interstate, something not so routine happened. Suddenly, I had a very strong impression to pray for God's safety and protection over myself and the truck I was driving. The weight of the experience felt heavy and serious—even urgent. It was an inner alert unlike anything I'd been through before. As you would expect a Jesus Moment to do, it definitely got my attention. As the Bible directs, I asked for the Lord to send His angels to take charge and surround me on the drive ahead. By the time I finished praying, I could sense His peaceful presence riding shotgun.

As it turned out, the ride was otherwise uneventful. I arrived in one piece, hopped out of the truck, and handed the keys to the grease monkey who would pull it around back for the work. Before he did, the guy checked the car over and then returned to where I was standing in conversation with our mechanic friend. The young man held three of the four lug nuts from one wheel in his hand and a look of utter disbelief on his face. "Mister," he said as he shook his head in amazement, "I don't know how you got here. Someone must have been looking out for you. You got here with three of these lug nuts nearly sheared off completely. The fourth broke off in my hand. You need to thank Someone upstairs for watching over you." Both mechanics looked at the pieces of broken metal, logically recognizing that what was there should not have held the wheel on my truck's axel. (Mind you, I had been traveling at around seventy miles per hour most of the way.)

We were all dumbstruck as the impact of what had just *not* happened began to settle in. With goose bumps tickling my arms and the hair on the back of my neck at full attention, I now understood the urgency of what I'd been prompted to pray at the beginning of my drive. My stomach dropped. For a moment we all just stood there in solemn awe. Then my heart soared. I explained what my heavenly Father had done. God is *so* incredible! I felt like starting a pep rally to fire up the crowd of people waiting in the service lounge. Did *they* know how He amazingly cares for us all?! Right then, these two mechanics and I sure did! All three of us celebrated the astonishing way He had watched over and protected me with each revolution of that wheel. In both dramatic examples like this and quieter moments, I'm thankful to know how to practice His presence and share Jesus Stories.

7 *Quieting to Connect*

My body is the original and primary place of my dominion and my responsibility. It is only through it that I have a world in which to live. That is why it, and not other physical objects in my world, is part of who I am and is essential to my identity. My life experiences come to me through or in conjunction with my body.

—DALLAS WILLARD

When I get stressed, I've learned to use my body to my advantage. Nothing fancy. Sometimes it means I breathe in God's presence and breathe out my frustration, fear, or anxiety; others times I invite a touch from God, as I focus and breathe out tension or pain. It's a matter of where I put my focus.

Some people love to work amidst distractions, constant interruptions, and noise. I envy their level of focus, but I'm not one of them. In fact, I'm not positive about this, but I think my brain's "default mode" is solitude. (Sometimes I wonder, with tongue firmly planted in cheek, *Should I be concerned?*)

Because I'm in the middle of writing this book, this is on my mind a lot lately. Some authors can write anywhere. I've observed that for me it takes a fair amount of time to get past a stilted, mechanical effort and into a flow. Honestly, sometimes it can take me hours to get there. All it takes is a quiet space and some predictable solitude. Then my keyboard begins to sing. It's great!

Maritza is joyful and enthusiastic. She loves to be with me. I feel the same—except when I'm in a writing groove. When that happens, she comes into the room excited to share her joy and connect, and then—like a planned reservoir release—my writing flow is drained and gone. I used to take great internal offense at these disturbances, thinking to myself, *I was just getting going! It took most of my day to find this productive headspace, and* now *you want to talk to me about something?*

One such day, just as I began to find words, there she was—the darling cork to my proverbial flow of words. Since becoming more aware of how interruptions like these were frustrating me, I had been working on ways to quiet myself down when they did occur. The more I practiced, the more I noticed that I was getting better at being able to relax. This day, rather than getting tense and aggravated, I sat there and thought to myself, *Ed, just breathe.* As Maritza began to talk, I don't think I understood a thing she was saying. *Breathe, Ed, just breathe.*

Suddenly, her words began to make sense. I was truly glad to see her—despite the interruption. Learning to quiet my body has allowed me to connect joyfully with her even when I've got important things to do. By breathing deeply and paying attention to the tension in my body, I have learned to stay relaxed, keep my mouth shut, and—most importantly—stay connected to the person I love more than anyone on the planet.

Until I started telling stories about this, Maritza had no idea I was "Quieting to Connect" with her in this way. This helpful training activity helped me prioritize our relationship over my problem of staying in a creative groove. In this and other practical ways, quieting benefits our relationship.

We Must Quiet to Connect

In my experience, Christians have resistance to describing and connecting with body sensations. Without much thought to the ramifications, many of us have gotten the message that what our body feels and wants is scary. Sometimes the message is subtle; other times it is outrageously overt. In both cases, the implication is that since our body is going to die, everything associated with it is too. It will only get us into trouble in the meantime. Along this line, the story goes, it is more spiritual—and way "safer"—to ignore our unsanctified, physical nature. Do you know what that means? Essentially, this way of thinking turns you and me into zombies—rotting corpses that move around unredeemed until we leave this earthly realm.

Brace yourself, fellow Christian, as this may strike you as counter to almost everything you and I have been told: your body is not your enemy.

The truth is quite the opposite, as a matter of fact. Our body is a powerful ally in the lifelong process of individual apprenticeship with Jesus. Like warning lights on the dashboard of our being, muscle tension, breathing, heart rate, and negative emotions can signal things that you and I can—and should—tend to. If we don't create margin in good times and then pay attention to these signals when we are under stress, you and I will find it difficult to deeply and sustainably connect with God—let alone with one another. Physically, emotionally, mentally, and spiritually, ignoring such internal noise makes our souls and Christian communities sick.

Earlier along my career path, I was a police officer. As part of that job, we were all required to complete regular in-service training. One such training involved judo. The other officers and I paired up for the drills. Unfortunately, I was placed with a guy who was at least fifty pounds heavier. I could have panicked, but thankfully I recognized the physics involved in the sport. Done right, judo doesn't have to hurt anyone. I tested out my theory against my fellow officer and lived to tell.

The name of the judo game is to leverage your opponent's momentum and use it against them. Law enforcement officers use it as a means of throwing bad guys off balance in order to gain control and take them into custody. Like bodily feelings and emotions, if we ignore an aggressive individual, they will overtake us. But if we flip their momentum, we can subdue their energy and regain the upper hand.

Whether you and I are conscious of it or not, if we don't pay attention to our body, eventually it will take its toll. A recent article in *Time Magazine* explains the physical effects: "Current neuroscience suggests that the more emotions and conflicts a person experiences, the more anxiety they feel. That's due, in part, to the vagus nerve, one of the main emotional centers of the body. It responds to emotions triggered in the mid-brain by sending signals to the heart, lungs, and intestines. These signals ready the body to take appropriate and immediate action in the service of survival. The body is ready to react to perceived danger before the person is aware that an emotion has been triggered."[15]

Negatively triggered, our bodies release hormones and neurotransmitters that amp us up. Left to these "devices," we become problem- or pain-centered in our thinking. As emotional intensity spikes, our relationships flounder in the wake. That is why practicing quiet and rest are so important. Quieting ourselves interrupts whatever level of upset we suffer and helps us to reconnect. In difficult situations, quieting activities help us calm down so we can get Jesus' perspective and ideas. For obvious reasons, you and I are well-advised to incorporate them into our days.

REASONS WHY QUIET AND REST HELP US

If we truly want to connect, these activities should be staples in our lives—and the lives of our small groups. If you still find yourself unconvinced, God has given us several reasons why quiet and rest help us connect:

Reason 1: The Connection Between Quiet and Calm

According to Scripture, being silent or still helps us to focus on (literally "to match") another. Our objective with the Quieting to Connect activity is to slow our reactions down enough so that we can engage with God and match his peaceful presence. When my focus is on God—outside myself—the ground that may have once felt all uphill becomes leveled.

Psalm 131:1–2 says, "My heart is not proud, LORD, my eyes are not haughty; I do not concern myself with great matters or things too wonderful for me. But I have calmed and quieted myself, I am like a weaned child with its mother; like a weaned child I am content." Snuggling into the presence of God, you and I will find the peace and contentment of a weaned child. Here, our lives are held, provided for, and comforted in God. Despite life's stresses, we are sure to find Him to be our faithful strength, refuge, and dwelling place (Psalm 1:3; 4:3–8; 62:5–8).

Reason 2: The Connection Between Quiet and Confidence

To be quieted is to assume a posture—an inner state of peace. This posture is resourced by trust and an assurance that the Holy Spirit's righteousness is in residence. (The alternative is a kind of skeptical distrust.) Together, when we share a healthy state of quiet with others in our group, we build trust. Confident of God's protection, you and I are able to abide in safety.

Isaiah 32:15–18 describes the lush, enduring confidence you and I enjoy when we are in this state, when "the Spirit is poured on us from on high, and the desert becomes a fertile field, and the fertile field seems like a forest. The LORD's justice will dwell in the desert, his righteousness live in the fertile field. The fruit of that righteousness will be peace; its effect will be quietness and confidence forever. My people will live in peaceful dwelling places, in secure homes, in undisturbed places of rest."

When we quiet to connect with God, we hear Him, see things from His perspective—and find ourselves better able to deal with fear (Isaiah 7:2–7; 14:3–7; Jeremiah 30:10–11). Instead, in practical ways, you and I can rest assured that quieting

- is a correct response to fear
- represents the opposite of fear
- banishes fear

Reason 3: Our Bodies Belong to Jesus

The Bible tells us a couple of things: 1) our bodies belong to the Lord, and 2) we are members of the body of Christ. As 1 Corinthians 6:19–20 tells us, "Do you not know that your bodies are temples of the Holy Spirit, who is in you, whom you have received from God? You are not your own; you were bought at a price. Therefore honor God with your bodies." Our bodies are to be a living sacrifice. As Paul emphasizes, "Therefore, I urge you, brothers and sisters, in view of God's mercy, to offer your bodies as a living sacrifice, holy and pleasing to God—this is your true and proper worship. Do not conform to the pattern of this world, but be transformed by the renewing of your mind. Then you will be able to test and approve what God's will is—his good, pleasing and perfect will" (Romans 12:1–2).

The life of Jesus is proclaimed through our bodies and, as such, lived out in our lives. Our souls inhabit the whole of us, so as long as you and I are alive on Earth, we can never act apart from these containers of ours. They directly impact how we relate with God, others, and the world. On a really practical level, quieting includes our mouths too—especially when we are stressed (James 3:2–6). In more ways than one, this can protect us—and others—from all kinds of corruption.

Think of it this way: your body is like a car God loaned you. This vehicle transports us around in the world—empowering us to interact with others and join God in His work. You get to drive this car, but if you don't fill it with gas and complete routine maintenance as the owner has asked, eventually the car and your transportation arrangement will quit working. While we are here on Earth, you and I get the privilege of using these bodies of ours, but they don't belong to us. We must pay attention to the owner's manual and warning indicators that can light up our system, or else plan on an eventual breakdown.

SPEAKING OF BREAKDOWN . . .

I'd be remiss if I ignored an obvious concern some have about the practice of quieting. Religious or not, plenty of people practice it these days; however, for nonbelievers it is an emptying stillness they pursue—not the spiritual filling with Jesus that we are after. This "other kind" of self-actualizing mindfulness is described by Dr. Dan Siegel as seeking to regulate the flow of energy and information in our brain to build a sense of awareness.[16] Buddhists follow a concentration practice called *samatha*, which centers their attention on an object to create inner tranquility or calm. Mindfulness, self-actualization, and Buddhism each use similar inner-reflection techniques as a means of enlightening necessary choices and change. Their goal is to build a sense of presence and awareness in this *empty* state.

As followers of Jesus, we seek much more than this self-determined emptiness. While there are obvious similarities in getting us to be *present*, what you and I truly seek is to get with God in order to be filled *with His presence*. Unlike the quieting that mindfulness, self-actualization, and Buddhism may provide, when we Quiet to Connect we are after space to focus on—and room to listen to—God. As with all *Beyond Becoming* activities, the goal is to engage in an interpersonal relationship with God. Deep, relational connection with the Lord, helps us to

- hear Him and become aware of His presence
- offer ourselves to Him as an act of worship
- be led by His Spirit
- respond to Him in trust and not fear
- avoid sin by keeping our mouth, anger, fear and difficult emotions from guiding our behavior
- share stories that testify of His goodness
- notice enjoyable body sensations described in the Psalms, including joy, peace, rest, contentment, and more
- deepen life experiences through our God-given senses, through which we savor goodness—like the taste of a vanilla ice cream cone on a hot summer day; the marvelously powerful beauty of ocean waves crashing on a sandy shore; the delightful sound of a child's uncontainable laughter; the soft feel of a blanket wrapped around us as we warm ourselves by a fire pit in the evening; or the soft, pine-drenched smell of crisp mountain air.

When you and I practice Quieting to Connect, we guard space to be grateful to God for His presence as well as to be present to others in our lives and to ourselves. It enables us to reflect on the experiences of each day—big and little. In his day Socrates said, "An unexamined life is not worth living." What about in our day? Are you and I living in such a way that we are making space to hear His voice? Cultural norms, activity assessments, loneliness stats, and social media images express that many of our Christian lives are just too full of clatter to connect fully in our relationships.

If we value hearing the voice of God and effectually praying for people in our midst, you and I must cultivate the practices encouraged by the Growing Gratitude, Jesus Moment and Jesus Stories, and

Quieting to Connect activities. These are foundational for most of what will follow in the *Beyond Becoming* activities that remain.

Activity #3: Quieting to Connect

Quieting to Connect is a three-step process. First, we will practice deep breathing, with an awareness that Jesus is with us. Second, we will learn a technique that helps us scan and release tension from our bodies. Finally, we will reflect on the experience. Combined, these methods help us synchronize body and breath so that we can enjoy a profound and attentive state of quiet before God. By Quieting to Connect, you and I train ourselves to settle down with Immanuel, God with us, rather than to run wildly through the terrain of our emotional and physical landscape. Group leaders should demonstrate and verbally lead members through each step of this activity.

STEP 1: Breathing Instructions. Invite the presence of Jesus to be with you as you practice the following steps for the breath portion of the Quieting to Connect activity:

1. Sit or lie down in a comfortable position, supporting as little weight as possible.
2. Put your hand on your stomach and take a very deep breath—in through your nose to the count of 4.*
3. Hold it for another count of 4.*
4. Then, exhale through your mouth to a count of 4.*
5. Hold your lungs empty for another count of 4, before breathing in again.*

* Adapt the count as necessary for yourself and your group.

Notice: did your hand move as you inhaled and exhaled? (When you and I breathe deeply, we can feel our stomachs fill as our diaphragms expand with air.) Research indicates that this breathing cycle is optimal for quieting our body's central nervous system. Pay attention to that feeling as you practice taking a couple more deep breaths.

STEP 2: Muscle Relaxation Instructions. Continue to practice deep breathing at a rate that is comfortable for you. **(Important note before beginning: Never tighten any area that is injured or compromised.)** One by one, take each body part listed below under number 4 through the following progression twice:

1. Tighten and hold the muscles of your _____* until it starts to feel a little uncomfortable (see Muscle Group Progression list below), ideally to a count of three.
2. Rest as you take two deep breaths.
3. Repeat #1 for the next muscle group.
4. Relax those muscles as you practice two more deep breaths before beginning with the next body part.

   * Muscle Group Progression:
   a. face
   b. shoulders and chest
   c. left arm and hand
   d. right arm and hand
   e. stomach
   f. legs
   g. feet

Now continue to take some deep breaths as you scan your whole body. Check and see if there's any part that still feels tense. Then tighten the troublesome muscle group to a count of three before relaxing again, taking two more deep breaths.

Exhale as you notice how your body feels now.

STEP 3: Closing Instructions for Reflection

1. Take a moment to ask Jesus silently to help you become more aware of His presence. Wait briefly as you listen.

2. Now ask Jesus if there is anything He'd like you to know.

3. Consider: Did anything seem to shift internally? Do you notice any of the following?

    • I feel a sense of God's peaceful presence with me.

    • I feel more hopeful, peaceful, and content.

    • I feel ready to connect with other people, including those in my small group.

    • My breathing is deep and regular.

    • My muscles feel more relaxed.

    • My thoughts are not racing.

4. Break into groups of three and discuss your response to the reflection questions above.

For a downloadable version of this worksheet, visit
www.equippinghearts.com

Quieting to Connect: Rhonda's Story

We live in a neighborhood of beautiful old trees. Recently, a forty-foot cypress directly across from us uprooted and came crashing down, blocking our entire street. It was pretty scary. So much so, that when our next-door neighbor noticed *our* cypress tree leaning toward his house, he asked if we would consider having it removed. We agreed to talk to our "tree guy" and, to make a long story short, decided to elevate our neighborly relationship above the problem tree.

One of our main criteria was that the tree removal company had current insurance. I researched and found what seemed to be a reliable contractor to do the job. I made a great connection with the guy who came out to estimate the job. He was very personable and assured me that his company was covered. As we shook hands, he promised to have the documentation emailed when he got back to the office. No problem. No problem until it didn't come . . . and after another phone call to him, it still didn't come. I talked to several people at the business. Still no certificate. After many attempts and way more conversation than necessary, I began to lose trust. I *definitely* lost my sense of peace. Quickly, I began to regret the contract I'd signed.

By then, I tried to get quiet, but all I could think about were the problems I'd already experienced with them, possible ways to fix what was wrong, and the potential consequences that may result if I couldn't. I was so tense! I felt like these guys were going to rip us off if I didn't stay vigilant. My frustration and fear continued to grow. After what seemed like my hundredth call about what should have been a simple matter, a tension headache pounded the point home: these guys were jerks!

That evening when my husband, Bill, got home from work, he could tell things weren't good. His presence and concern began to help me calm down and realize I wasn't in this alone. He reminded me that Jesus was with us, and encouraged me to take some good deep breaths to quiet my body. Then, together we went to work on the issue. Between the two of us, we eventually managed to get the paperwork we needed from the tree removal company and the work could proceed at last.

Only at that point did I feel like I could confess the extent of my fears to Bill; then the *real* problem came to light. It was glaring! When I didn't get what I needed, the relational part of me had shut down. I had spiraled into fear and frustration. The whole experience taught me a valuable lesson in what to look for and listen for in my body and my emotions. And we were able to demonstrate our love for our neighbor at the same time! Should I ever be tempted to forget the importance of Quieting to Connect in the future, the yard space where our cypress tree once stood is a perfect reminder.

8 *Joining with Jesus*

I ask—ask the God of our Master, Jesus Christ, the God of glory—to make you intelligent and discerning in knowing him personally, your eyes focused and clear, so that you can see exactly what it is he is calling you to do, grasp the immensity of this glorious way of life he has for his followers, oh, the utter extravagance of his work in us who trust him—endless energy, boundless strength! All this energy issues from Christ: God raised him from death and set him on a throne in deep heaven, in charge of running the universe, everything from galaxies to governments, no name and no power exempt from his rule. And not just for the time being, but forever. He is in charge of it all, has the final word on everything.

—EPHESIANS 1:18–20 MSG

A while ago I was invited to speak at an addiction and trauma conference in Finland. The content we were dealing with tends to stir up deep issues for some people. Keeping that in mind, I was a little apprehensive when the organizers set up a line for people to come forward for prayer. I was a guest, however, and I did what I was asked.

At one point a woman named Leena stood in front of me and, with no detail, asked that I pray for her. *Whew! That I can do*, I thought. As is my practice when I pray for others, I began by quieting myself and asking Jesus how *He* was praying for her. Immediately an image flashed in my mind's eye. I saw her as a young girl or teen hiding under a dresser. It was kind of strange, so I hesitated and asked the Lord, *Jesus, is this You?* In my spirit I felt prompted to share the picture I'd been given.

Admitting that I wasn't sure what it meant, I told Leena what I'd seen. Right away, she burst into delighted laughter! "That is where I would hide when I was afraid as a little girl," she exclaimed. We talked for a while longer, and she shared how that scene reassured her that Jesus was with her all along. The specifics of the image confirmed for her that God knew her fear. She felt utterly seen and understood. I began to pray for her—thanking God that He was with Leena as a little girl, just as He is now. I asked that He would give her an ongoing and increasing awareness of His presence—especially at times when she may feel afraid. By the time we finished our brief conversation, Leena had concluded that if the Lord did that for her when she was a child, certainly He would do the same with her fears now.

What a beautiful outcome! See what the Lord did there? At that moment, through that image, Jesus masterfully harmonized His presence with the song of her life experience—bringing it all together.

What did I do? I simply shared a picture that came to me when I asked Jesus how I could join Him—then I got out of the way. In Leena's case, I wasn't even sure what the image meant—and that was okay. God affirmed His presence and understanding of her need. It was between the two of them. I was just an instrument of His grace.

IS JOINING WITH JESUS A BIBLICAL FORM OF PRAYER?

While Joining with Jesus and the language surrounding it may be new to you, Jesus showed us throughout the Word how it's to be done. The New Testament tells us we have a heavenly intercessor. As Romans 8:26–27 explains, "In the same way, the Spirit helps us in our weakness. We do not know what we ought to pray for, but the Spirit himself intercedes for us through wordless groans. And he who searches our hearts knows the mind of the Spirit, because the Spirit intercedes for God's people in accordance with the will of God."

A few lines later in verse 34, the chapter reassures us that Jesus is also in constant intercession with the Father on our behalf: "Who then is the one who condemns? No one. Christ Jesus who died—more than that, who was raised to life—is at the right hand of God and is also interceding for us." Another biblical source, Hebrews 7:25 (ESV), also confirms that Jesus is praying for us: "He is able to save to the uttermost those who draw near to God through him, since he always lives to make intercession for them."

Jesus is our model, our Master. So, the idea that we pray for one another just makes sense. As He demonstrated, though, prayer works best when done in accordance with God's will—not our own. The distinction I'm trying to make lies in the source and origin of our intercession. We are wise to ask *Him* how *He* is praying before we begin.

An intercessor is just a person who intervenes in prayer on someone else's behalf. On Earth, it's a privilege to fill the role for each other. God can use a lot of different ways to communicate with you, me, and those in our small groups. His voice may break through in Scripture, with a word(s), using a story, or conveyed in a strong feeling or impression. Remember, as we learn to adopt this practice, we are simply asking God how He is praying for a person—right now, before we dive in. The idea that Jesus would want to share His prayers with us seems obvious.

Ultimately, praying this way is a test of our humility. It keeps us from forgetting that we are not the star of the show. The spotlight needs to be on Him and Him alone. Whatever you and I do in the process of praying with Jesus for others, we should never attempt to steal the limelight or assume we are speaking for Him. Remember: you and I are *joining* Him in what He is up to.

If you ask Jesus and nothing comes to mind, just ask God what the person has asked you to pray for, or think of blessings from the Bible that would bless them in their expressed need. In the words of philosopher Dallas Willard, "To bless is to will the good of another." We can at least do this!

JOINING WITH JESUS IS *NOT* GENERIC

When we were taught to pray in a small group setting, most of us learned a pretty generic format. According to these popular group prayer methods, everyone should share their needs one at a time. If something big was going down—an illness, a job loss, a wayward child—the group would organize itself around the pain or crisis. We learned to gear prayer around our needs—specifically, around meeting them. Now, don't get me wrong: it is not bad to pray for specific needs. However, when we let problems or pain become the focus of our prayer, it limits us.

Starting here, do we allow ourselves to think about how Jesus wants us to pray? Are you and I in the habit of asking Jesus how He may want us to address an issue? When we do, prayer becomes much more than a duty or a compassionate response to needs and pain. Our prayers reflect His agenda. As we seek the Lord's presence and direction in a situation or circumstance *before* we pray, it can change everything. One thing is for sure: when we pray with God's possibilities, it becomes a whole lot more fun!

For some, this may sound like I am taking you wading in charismatic waters without a life jacket. If this is you, I understand. Unsure how to swim, you may not feel safe—heck, you may not even be sure you *want* to. Let me encourage you, this kind of prayer *is* your life jacket. Using Scripture as our lifeguard, this method helps us learn to pray the same way Jesus is praying. When we do, group prayer times become about listening and responding to Him.

Activity #4: Joining with Jesus

One of the many great aspects of the Joining with Jesus activity is that it can be added at *almost* any point in your small group . . . just not at the very beginning of your meeting. Why? Well, we want to first experience and establish a sense of God's presence and be able to interact with Him—both individually and as a group—*before* we start praying together. That being said, starting with Growing Gratitude (Chapter 5), Jesus Moments and Jesus Stories (Chapter 6), Quieting to Connect (Chapter 7), Scripture Reflection (Chapter 9), or Conversation with Jesus (Chapter 10) sets a great foundation for this practice. Any of these activities safeguard a meeting from being more driven by the intensity of pain or problems than by God. Reactions to such stressors will quickly hijack our attention.

(Note to group leaders: Ideally, I suggest doing the Joining with Jesus activity at the end of your time together in groups of three. Depending on time and the size of your group, you can opt to do it with your entire group. Begin by asking group members if they have prayer requests.)

1. After each person is given a chance to share, allow group members time to pray for one another.
2. Before beginning to pray aloud, give everyone time to quiet and connect with Jesus. Once group members have had a chance to be still for a moment, remind each person to ask, "Jesus, how are you praying for _____ [insert individual's name here] right now?" Pay attention to what comes to mind. Notice any words, scriptures, thoughts, feelings, pictures, or impressions you receive.

3. Once you've quieted and listened, then pray for the individual
    aloud, keeping in mind the following guidelines:

    •   **Honor and respect the person you are praying
        for.** We are joining hearts and voices to intercede
        for them—not to demonstrate our giftedness. Prayer
        requests are very personal. As such, treat those with
        incredible honor and respect. People are being
        vulnerable when they express their weaknesses, needs,
        desires, hopes, and dreams. Praying for others means
        being invited to join them in a deep place in their life.
        Treat it reverently.

    •   **Pray what you hear from the Lord—don't explain
        it.** Base it upon your impressions from God and the
        need that has been expressed. It is not necessary to
        explain all the thoughts, images, impressions, or
        scriptures that may have come to mind. I've been in
        groups where people have gone into such elaborate
        and lengthy detail that it derails everyone's focus. You
        can tell when that happens because suddenly prayer
        time becomes a platform for the person praying to
        soft-brag about their gifting.

    •   **Never presume to be speaking for God.** In this activity,
        we are praying *with* Jesus, not speaking *for* Him. In my
        experience, some people have a great deal of difficulty
        praying without prefacing it with "The Lord told me
        . . ." or "God says . . ." Either of these stances will put
        the person being prayed for in an awkward position.
        Such a prayer is issued more like a divine proclamation
        and leaves the individual with little choice whether to
        agree or remain silent. (Honestly, how do you argue
        with God about something He may or may not have

said through another person?) By praying instead of pronouncing, the individual being prayed over has the opportunity to receive your words and talk with God. Always help one another listen to God for themselves.

- **Avoid hazards.** Spiritual gifts are handled differently among Christian fellowships and denominations. If you don't know your group members well or if they come from different backgrounds, this is important to consider. Establish a safe environment by steering clear of any unnecessary offense.

- **Joining with Jesus is intended to strengthen, encourage, and comfort.** It is not the time to confront or rebuke.

- **When in doubt, bless with Scripture.** Share generic verses that you are certain will provide comfort or peace.

- **Do not offer opinions, advice, or medical information, and don't tell people what to do.** Any of these will be off-putting or even offensive—the opposite of relational grace.

- **Recognize the limitations of a small group setting.** This activity is not the right place to attempt to address a person's deep wounds or to start a process of "inner healing" for the individual.

Joining with Jesus: Gretta's Story

I think I was born a community organizer. Advocating for those who don't have a voice lights me up! Often the needs these groups face are overwhelming—even urgent—so my background in crisis management has proved a great asset. Those are the times I'm especially thankful that I was introduced to the Joining with Jesus activity! It has changed the way I pray, and it's been a lifeline for me and those I serve.

Along that line, I am part of a group that gets together regularly to pray. One such time, I *really* needed it! Things had heated up around a particular policy that directly affected some groups that I've worked with as a consultant. I'll admit that while I have a lot of expertise in this specific area, nothing in my PhD program prepared me for how to deal with the ramifications of what was going on (or the number of text messages blowing up my phone in the middle of our prayer time). I was getting a lot of pressure to "sound the alarm" and publicly address the issue. Basically, I was being told, "Gretta, this is an emergency! You've got to fix this for us!" The pressure and anxiety grew with every *ping* of my phone. *Am I supposed to get involved with this thing? —and, if so,* how? I wondered. This required the Lord's wisdom, so I asked for prayer regarding how to respond. Together, our prayer group spent time Quieting to Connect before moving on to Joining with Jesus in prayer.

Honestly, the time waiting on Jesus changed everything. As she asked the Lord how He was praying for me, my friend Molly saw a picture of glassy-still water. Immediately, she made the connection to Psalm 23 and the way God led David by still waters to rest and restore his soul. That became Molly's prayer for me—that Jesus would help me find the still waters and be able to rest with Him. It was such a gift!

Along with the clarity of the image, the prayer resonated deep within me, but still my blasted phone kept distracting me with alerts from my office. (People were continuing to panic!) As if oblivious to the racket, Molly persisted in prayer. Suddenly, the clamor in my thoughts went away, and the sense of fear I'd felt settled down. The anxiety and stress left me. In their place, I found Jesus was with me, leading me to a place of peace where His presence would deeply restore me. I was able to quiet my spirit and rest with Him. I was able to ask Him how to respond to the situation at work. Soon I heard *His* answer. With great peace, I knew that this was one crisis I was not called to manage. I directed all those concerned to a colleague I highly esteem (and, truth be told, he is an even better fit for the job than I). Predictably, God knew the best possible solution and just how to pray it into being!

9 *Scripture Reflection and Spoken-Word Reflection*

When Scripture shapes our thoughts, we are more likely to act on it. Because this meditation occurs in a relaxed everyday setting, the truth is more likely to become embedded in everyday thoughts and actions. —JAN JOHNSON

"Jesus with His Friend" (Seventh-century Coptic icon, Egypt)

Remember Show and Tell time at school? What I want to do next is kind of like that. You see, teaching *Beyond Becoming* activities for so long, I have learned it is easier to show some of them than to try to tell about them. In part, that is because a lot of us have preconceived notions about what Scripture Reflection is (or is *not*). So, before you and I presume to be on the same page, let me share a story about a leader training class I recently taught on the subject.

In one particular class, I was teaching *Beyond Becoming* to about a dozen small group leaders. As soon as everyone arrived that Saturday, we prayed for the meeting and settled in, spending some time Quieting to Connect with Jesus. After there was a sense that His peace was "in the building," we began talking about how the Lord had shown up in our respective lives since the last time our group had met (aka Jesus Stories). Without question, the group recognized His joyful presence among us before we moved into the focus of our meeting: learning to practice the Scripture Reflection activity together. Again, we prayed, inviting the Lord to guide whatever came next.

Then I pulled out my journal, opened my Bible, and began the exercise along with the class. Unhurried, I read through the passage once in order to understand what it was about.

The passage was Ephesians 2:1–9 (NKJV), which reads,

And you *He made alive*, who were dead in trespasses and sins, in which you once walked according to the course of this world, according to the prince of the power of the air, the spirit who now works in the sons of disobedience, among whom also we all once conducted ourselves in the lusts of our flesh, fulfilling the desires of the flesh and of the mind, and were by nature children of wrath, just as the others.

But God, who is rich in mercy, because of His great love with
which He loved us, even when we were dead in trespasses,
made us alive together with Christ (by grace you have been
saved), and raised *us* up together, and made *us* sit together in
the heavenly *places* in Christ Jesus, that in the ages to come He
might show the exceeding riches of His grace in *His* kindness
toward us in Christ Jesus. For by grace you have been saved
through faith, and that not of yourselves; *it is* the gift of God,
not of works, lest anyone should boast.

I love God's Word, so modeling this activity is easy. I don't have
some canned journaling thing from long ago. When I teach the Scripture
Reflection activity, I sincerely enjoy taking a fresh read and a new listen
to anything the Word has for me. On this day, as always, I poured over
the passage along with everyone else.

After gathering the gist from an initial read through the passage,
I went back to the beginning and started to read it through again,
this time paying attention to any words or phrases that jumped out
at me. Well, this time I made it no further than "And you" (yes, *really*.)
Right off the bat, it was as if the Lord had taken a Sharpie marker
and drawn a heavy black circle around these two words as if to say, "Hey,
Ed, I'm not talking to some other random person reading. I'm talking
to *you*, personally, about what follows. *You* have my full attention *right
now*."

Our conversation continued as I asked Him, "So what do you want
me to know about how this relates to me personally, Jesus?"

He replied, "Of all the people I've written this for, I want *you* to
know how much I care for *you*. I died for *you*." Evidently, God knew
my soul needed to hear that afresh. *I knew* it was important to take the
time to hear *and receive* what He had quickened to my attention. All of
a sudden, the whole passage was about *me*—I was at the center of the

story, not a distant observer. As He drew me in, my heart rate went up a bit with anticipation. I read on . . .

Three more words: "He made alive." He. Made. *Alive*. Alive is what hooked me, this time. Again I asked, "What is it you want me to know about 'alive,' Lord?"

"Ed, I made you alive—*at this very time and in this very place—to help you connect with the life of God around you. Look closely and you'll recognize more of life in Me through My creation. It's all around you!"* Clearly, the Lord longs for me to deeply experience the richness of my *life*—not all the extraneous things that compete for my attention. Just as I recognized that idea, a rush of thoughts and images flooded my senses: things like the rustle of birds singing in the bushes just outside my window; freshly verdant North Carolina views where I live; craggy high-altitude wonders I've experienced in Colorado's Rocky Mountains; and the joy-laced fullness of life with Maritza, my children, and theirs. The life that God has given me *is* overflowing with goodness and grace!

Feeling the depth of God's love for me, I posed one more question: "Jesus, why do you want me to know that, especially, right now?"

"I want you to soak that in because I know the demands that are on you and your time. I don't want you to miss what I made for you to enjoy. Savor your life as it is expressed in everyone and everything I have made. I had you in mind when I formed each one. This is life. It is fuel for what I've called you to do. I made you alive to focus on these things for life—not the things that the world will try to use as distractions."

Frequently, a phrase will jump out at me or a word will leap off the page like that. After it seems like I've listened to the Lord's prompting, I may decide to grab a Bible commentary or a lexicon and dig a little deeper. All the while, I keep in mind that the purpose of the Scripture Reflection activity is to engage with God through His Word. Otherwise, it's easy to wander off on a study trip. Again, engage with your heart, don't just study with your head. John 5:39–40 says that Jesus chided Jewish religious leaders, saying, "You study the Scriptures diligently because you think that in them you have eternal life. These are the very Scriptures that testify about me, yet you refuse to come to me to have life."

If you want the life Jesus is referring to, first come to Him—connect with Him! Then remember, this (and every other *Beyond Becoming* activity) is intended to establish grace-based attachment with others in your small group too. When you meet, be with God together and share in real time.

That can happen when you and I start at the beginning. By paying attention to the Holy Spirit's leading in this way, you and I contemplate the Word and it is "made flesh" in our very own lives. Jesus dwells among us and speaks to us in unique and inescapable ways. There is no discussion, comparing notes, or teaching during this portion of the exercise. (There will be time for that later, during the group sharing time.) With holy curiosity as our guide, you and I ask questions like "What do you want to show me, God?" or "Jesus, why do you want me to know that right now?"

MORE THAN YOUR BASIC BIBLE STUDY

By now, I'd guess that you are clear what I mean by Scripture Reflection. Studying the Word for historical, cultural, archeological, or linguistic purposes is interesting—even enlightening—but apart from a relationship with its divine author, our character will remain unchanged in any sustainable way. Studying the Bible for knowledge is good, but there is more available to us than reading for information. Engaging with God and others is part of the process that transforms us. There is a distinction between what we are doing with this exercise versus what many of us have been taught is "enough" in our life with God.

A NONNEGOTIABLE FOR SPIRITUAL GROWTH

In case I've been unclear up until now, if you want to grow to be more like Christ, you must *engage* with Scripture. Engaging implies personal interaction with the Word. Research indicates that it is nonnegotiable—spiritual maturity just can't happen otherwise. With that in mind, grab your Bible, a journal or notebook, and something to write with. Let's get started.

Activity #5: Scripture Reflection

As before, keep a couple of important things in mind as you listen to God through His Word:

- Thoughts and impressions that you and I journal do not carry the same authority as Scripture.
- During your reflection time, if you need help distinguishing what God's thoughts might be, see the list provided in the article "Is the Shepherd Speaking?" You will find it in the Appendix.

For this exercise, each person will need a Bible, a notebook or journal, and a pen to record their insights. Allow 10–15 minutes for everyone to reflect independently on the selected passage. While you may remain in the same room, you and your group members should spend this time *on your own,* silently reading, listening for Jesus' voice, and asking Him questions about it. Do not share your insights with anyone until the time is complete. You will have time to share your reflections during the group discussion that follows.

1. If you haven't already done a *Beyond Becoming* activity to welcome God's presence among you (that is, any of those found in chapters 5, 6, and 7), take a moment to remember something you appreciate or a specific time you have felt deeply connected to God. Reflect on the time, remembering how it made you feel. Take a few deep breaths before continuing.

2. Pray and ask Jesus to guide you as you reflect on the selected passage of Scripture.

3. To get an overview, read through the whole passage once.

4. Slowly read the passage of Scripture a second time. As you read, pay attention to any words or phrases that seem to jump out at you. Note each in your journal.

5. Then, stop and ask Jesus what He wants you to know about the word(s) or phrase(s). After you ask, pay attention to any thoughts, feelings, impressions, pictures, memories, or other scriptures that come to mind and write them in your journal.

6. After you've finished journaling your observations, pray over them. Ask Jesus to show you if there is anything more that He may want you to know about what you've written. Enter these in your journal.

7. If you have the time, continue reading the passage of Scripture, journaling and interacting with Jesus.

8. Once you have finished journaling, read through all you have written. Think about what you have learned from this scripture that applies to your life right now. Pray over it, asking the Lord to guide you. Maybe there is a theme or key lesson that speaks to your heart; perhaps God is calling you to action or further reflection. Write these observations in your journal.

**For a downloadable version of this worksheet, visit
www.equippinghearts.com**

Sharing: Right-of-Way Rules for You and Your Group

I hope by now you see the essential nature of sharing your God-given insights This is not an optional part of the practice and should not be considered an "add-on if there's time." Rather, this is where the rubber meets the relational road. There are numerous benefits to sharing with our small groups (most of which we covered earlier). Though it may feel uncomfortable at first, when we listen to God, it helps us to grow a deeper more interactive relationship with Him. The same can be said of sharing with others. Sharing allows people to acquire a deeper understanding of each other. When you and I reveal our hearts, we can be more fully seen, heard, known, and companioned by God and others. Our grace-based attachments are built and strengthened. We grow together! That only happens when we open up.

As you share, here are some guidelines to help keep you and your group members safely in your own lanes:

- When it's your turn to share, ask your group for feedback to help you get better at recognizing the Shepherd's voice.
- Listen supportively. Never offer criticism or unsolicited advice or opinions.
- Keep in mind that your collective goal is to help each other better recognize when Jesus is interacting with each person.
- Refer to "Is the Shepherd Speaking?" to guide and limit your feedback.
- Graciously point out the consistencies—or inconsistencies—that you notice.
- Offer feedback that helps each group member better connect with God.

For a downloadable version of this worksheet, visit
www.equippinghearts.com

Sharing Your Scripture Reflection with Others

Allow each person two to three minutes to share their reflections on the selected Scripture passage. Depending on the size of your group, you may choose to stay together or break into groups of three in order to give each person adequate time. This should take no more than ten to fifteen minutes of your total meeting time.

AS YOU GO . . .

Remember to apply your Scripture Reflection this week. Following your small group meeting, set aside additional time to reflect on what you have gleaned. Continue journaling about it. Ask the Lord if He has deeper insights to share with you. You may want to dig into the passage further—studying more deeply using the help of biblical commentary, a concordance, or teachings on specific topics left unaddressed due to time constraints. Continue to join God in your Scripture Reflection as you watch for Jesus Stories to unfold in your life.

Beyond Becoming: A Group Experience

Recently, I took some leaders through the Group Scripture Reflection activity using Psalm 84. Here it is for your review:

> How lovely is your dwelling place,
>   Lord Almighty!
> My soul yearns, even faints,
>   for the courts of the Lord;
> my heart and my flesh cry out
>   for the living God.
> Even the sparrow has found a home
>   and the swallow a nest for herself,
>   where she may have her young—
> a place near your altar,

LORD Almighty, my King and my God.
Blessed are those who dwell in your house;
>   they are ever praising you.

Blessed are those whose strength is in you,
>   Whose hearts are set on a pilgrimage.
As they pass through the Valley of Baka,
>   they make it a place of springs;
>   the autumn rains also cover it with pools.
They go from strength to strength,
>   till each appears before God in Zion.

Hear my prayer, LORD God Almighty;
>   listen to me, God of Jacob.
Look on our shield, O God;
>   Look with favor on your anointed one.

Better is one day in your courts
>   than a thousand elsewhere;
I would rather be a doorkeeper in the house of my God
>   than dwell in the tents of the wicked.
For the LORD God is a sun and shield;
>   the LORD bestows favor and honor;
no good thing does he withhold
>   from those whose walk is blameless.

LORD Almighty,
>   blessed is the one who trusts in you.

After allowing ample time to engage with God through the passage,
I asked volunteers from the group to share their insights.

Liza: Psalm 84 brought to mind my past fifteen years—dwelling, praising, and living like a sparrow in my little nest. Then, verse 6 got me! When it spoke about how the faithful pass through the Valley of Baka, I remembered that "Baka" is the word for tears or weeping. My mom just passed after a long illness. Without a doubt, my worst night of tears was the night before she died. The Lord used my tears like springs of water—it was as if He was cleansing my heart. When my sisters arrived, we spent time crying, praying, grieving together. The whole thing was incredibly healing. Since then I feel like I have been moving from strength to strength. From that place in the passage through the end, mentions of "Lord," "God," and "Almighty" made my soul feel like it was soaring. I can see how I've grown. At my lowest point, God showed up . . . like WOW! It was totally unexpected.

Caroline: The psalmist said, "My soul yearns and even faints for the living God." What an example of someone I want to be! I want that from the inside out! I want to be someone who lives right here in Scripture. Through that Valley, we will all appear before God in Zion. The Lord gives strength to help us make it. He wants intimacy with us and He gives the strength. It's not about me getting myself there.

Theressa: I work as a counselor. When people come to me for help, part of my job is to listen for what they *aren't* saying. The past few weeks have been especially busy. I've had a lot of tearful people in my office. As I was reflecting on this scripture, it turned out that my problem was not what I thought. I told the Lord, *I don't know what's going on!* He showed me that I'm trying to be strong for all these people and listen to them, but what God is saying is that I don't need to be *strong*. He wants me to be *well*. He reassured me that I can be well in the dwelling place He has made for me with Him. That is the yearning of my heart. The words that jumped out at me were "dwelling place," "strength to strength," "near," and "hear me, God." He said, *"You are blessed when you're near. I'm yearning for nearness."* Again, it was not the direction I thought we were going when we started the activity.

Lauren: I was reflecting on the progression of my soul in this passage. First, the psalmist talks about being captured by the beauty of the Lord—being with the Lord in His house. I thought to myself, *If the birds can get there, it must be easy.* Then, I went through the Valley of Tears. I've been to that place before, and I've seen and know His intimacy. I was quickly taken back to remember how God will bring those times of refreshment. It struck me: favor and honor don't come first. God honors those who *trust.* That only comes out of a place of spending time with Him in His house.

Lorenzo: I was taken by the promise that autumn rain will wash the Valley of Baka. It represents a forty-year experience for me. Finally, I think we are in the autumn rain. As I read the scripture, I also put a box around every mention of the word *blessed.* Look at them all [turning it so we could see, he held up his Bible]. I feel like I'm always asking, "What does it mean for Christ to be formed in a group. What should I look for to know that I'm on the right track?" The thing God showed me is *blessed* are those who dwell in your house. If praise is going on, then they must be in His house. Praise lives there. Obviously, praise-filled hearts are set on Him. If we are finding that strength, then we are people on that pilgrimage. "Blessed is the one who trusts in you." That tells me that the Lord God is bigger than any situation—there is an indication of trust in our relationship. I know to trust in that, even without all the answers.

See what we can learn with one another through Group Scripture Reflection? There is a big difference between this and a study where only one person teaches based exclusively on their learning and insight. An important part of learning the Bible, it is essential for our spiritual growth.

The whole idea is talking with God as we are engaging with His Word. From there, if you are led to pull out a lexicon and discover what "Baka" means in Hebrew, for instance, you are doing it as a response to God's leading. Our focus is not a mere quest for knowledge, in other words. There is nothing wrong with getting smarter about the Bible, but we are after more. We want spiritual transformation, not just spiritual information. We can ask questions. He can show us places where our thinking may be wrong.

A lot can be revealed as we listen to the Lord, His Word, and what He is teaching the people in our small group. His Word comes to life, and our lives come out in its light. God reveals a lot of His goodness. Experiencing Scripture together this way grows our attachment—as a group and with the Lord.

SPOKEN-WORD SCRIPTURE REFLECTION: AN ALTERNATIVE[17]

For a variety of reasons, sometimes Scripture Reflection is best done orally. Reading God's Word out loud may serve your purposes best. You could be serving a population that doesn't read and write well, in a culture that is accustomed to transmitting information through its generations by word of mouth, or perhaps your small group just needs to change up how they meditate on God's Word. Whatever the circumstance, Spoken-Word Scripture Reflection is a good tool to have in your toolbox if you want to help folks engage.

Several years ago, Maritza and I were invited to work with prison ministry in the South Pacific. I would be helping train their people to work with inmates recovering from addiction. Upon arrival, we were greeted by a man in uniform who interviewed us before expounding on the glories of their prison system. Once he was done, we were escorted to an open-air hut to meet the fifty to sixty volunteers we would be training. These were nationals with a heart to go into the prison. There were no Bibles and no guarantee that anyone could read in English—or any other language. We had a screen, a projector, and an audience.

Gratefully, before the visit our host briefed us about something that had happened the previous week. It seems a doctor had come in to train the same group and overwhelmed them with slides, handouts, and concepts that left them virtually overwhelmed. By the end, they were mentally fried. It stirred up feelings of embarrassment and shame that they were unable to understand and process all that had been presented. *We need to be careful with what and how we communicate,* I thought.

Once I caught a glimpse of the audience and the facility, the solution to effective, relational training was clear: we would teach them to tell stories as a means of helping these prisoners recover. You see, storytelling is an integral part of their culture. It flows out of them. Teaching them to incorporate into this tradition was life-giving for all concerned.

Here's how it is done.

1. Select a passage of Scripture to read aloud. (This process works exceptionally well with stories and parables from Scripture.)
2. Pray, asking God to engage the group's hearts and minds to hear His Word and imagine the scene.
3. Read through the verses slowly so everyone can hear and have ample time to absorb what is being said. Pause for a minute and then repeat—reading the passage in an unhurried fashion. When you are done with the reading, everyone should close their Bibles and set them aside.
4. Next, if your group is so large that the following process becomes cumbersome, break into small groups of at least three so that everyone has an opportunity to participate in the steps.
5. After reading slowly, give everyone a chance to retell the story they just heard to one another.

6. Once they are settled, explain that you will be guiding them through a short series of reflection questions. For each one, they will have ten minutes to share their responses among themselves before the next question is posed. Remind them
   • to make sure everyone has a chance to share their reflections
   • to use the time to learn with and from one another, not to critique or teach

7. Then guide them through the following questions:
   • What do you think was in God's mind?
   • Why did He want us to know that?
   • Where is the grace in this story?

8. If there is time, allow one person from each group to summarize the key insights from their sharing time with the larger group. Once this is done, affirm how many good things God is able to teach us through one another.

For a downloadable version of this worksheet, visit
www.equippinghearts.com

SOME TAKEAWAYS FROM A RECENT SPOKEN-WORD SCRIPTURE REFLECTION

As with traditional Scripture Reflection, remember to apply what you've learned from this Spoken-Word Reflection. Following your small group meeting, make time to contemplate the conversation some more. Continue journaling about it. Ask the Lord if He has even deeper discernment to offer you. You may also want to seek wisdom from your small group leader or pastor about specific topics or questions that you're led to explore. Then, watch how God's Word takes root in your life story.

Scripture Reflection: A Group Experience

During a recent leader training class, we reviewed Spoken-Word Scripture Reflection using Matthew 22:1–14. First, I read it aloud to them:

> Jesus spoke to them again in parables, saying: "The kingdom of heaven is like a king who prepared a wedding banquet for his son. He sent his servants to those who had been invited to the banquet to tell them to come, but they refused to come.

> "Then he sent some more servants and said, 'Tell those who have been invited that I have prepared my dinner: My oxen and fattened cattle have been butchered, and everything is ready. Come to the wedding banquet.'

> "But they paid no attention and went off—one to his field, another to his business. The rest seized his servants, mistreated them and killed them. The king was enraged. He sent his army and destroyed those murderers and burned their city.

> "Then he said to his servants, 'The wedding banquet is ready, but those I invited did not deserve to come. So go to the street corners and invite to the banquet anyone you find.' So the servants went out into the streets and gathered all the people they could find, the bad as well as the good, and the wedding hall was filled with guests.

> "But when the king came in to see the guests, he noticed a man there who was not wearing wedding clothes. He asked, 'How did you get in here without wedding clothes, friend?'

The man was speechless.

"Then the king told the attendants, 'Tie him hand and foot, and throw him outside, into the darkness, where there will be weeping and gnashing of teeth.'

"For many are invited, but few are chosen."

After allowing each person to retell the passage in their own words, we dove into the exercise. The following is a transcript of our dialogue:

Ed (assuming the role of group leader): So, what do you think was in God's mind when He gave us that story? Why would He want us to know that? [Pausing to give them time to reflect, before asking each of them to share their responses with the group.] So again, what do you think was in God's mind and why would He want us to know that?

Pete: I think it's about having reverence and respect for God as well as a desire to not offend or hurt the host. He went to a lot of trouble to prepare for the occasion. That was a lot back then! He couldn't just run to the grocery store for the ingredients. To have love and compassion for His effort and generosity is the right thing to do. I know some people think the part throwing the guy out into the darkness may seem harsh, but God is demonstrating that when we don't appreciate what He is offering, there is consequence involved.

Dan: I think it's all about preparation. Other places in Scripture, He calls us the Bride of Christ and allows us to start setting our heart right throughout our lives—not at just one salvation point in time. Being fake or lukewarm won't cut it. We've got to put in the effort in as needed along the way and as God intended. It is an open invitation to all of us to experience and enjoy that relationship together. He wants us to grow in Him and grow in love together.

Jim: To me, the wedding feast is kind of like the price that Jesus paid for the invitation to everyone. It's the preparation that God made back then. When Jesus came to the religious group of His day, He said it's not the stuff you can bring or what you can do that will get you into the party. It's what *He* did, what *He* gave you to put on. (I learned once that a wealthy host would even provide people with the proper wedding clothes they needed to attend. It takes emptying yourself—putting on God's best from the inside out. That is the only thing that shows you, me, and everyone else that we are on His list. You can't see inside a person. But that day when the host's eyes are on you, *He* will see. You and I can't just wear the clothes *we* want or earn.

Mary Beth: I really love that passage because to me it's a picture of the Father's heart to want to celebrate real union with us. It shows us joy and the contrast of the reality of what happens when we do not respond to God on His terms. He is our Host. It's not an employer-employee or a slave-master relationship. It is a story about a Father wanting to celebrate His Son's union. He is celebrating the maturity of that son to take a bride home to the Father's house. To me, that is a real picture of Church.

Ed: So where did you notice grace in the story?

Pete: I may be wrong, but I think I remember God not getting a response from the people He first invited. In the end, didn't He send his servants to bring people He didn't even know? *That* was grace.

Dan: He dressed the undressed guest. The guy had one shot, he messed up. Then, God gave him another.

Jim: I saw God's grace in the fact that those who ended up attending the party weren't the "A-List." The people who were gathered *outside* the gates trying to see who was attending ended up being invited inside.

Mary Beth: God is making a statement, I think, about the next generation making it. Family is important to Him. Love is important no matter what everyone else stands for. I like that part. My dad was always great at welcoming guests and celebrating family. I saw that happen at home . . . he was a great host.

As we wrapped up the activity, I pointed out the simplicity of what they had just experienced. "See? Spoken-Word Reflection is not hard," I told them. "*And* what each of us contributes enriches our connection—with God and each other. Do you see how differently God is at work in your lives through the same passage? I feel like I know each of you a little better too."

10 *Conversation with Jesus*

We may ignore, but we can nowhere evade the presence of God. The world is crowded with Him. He walks everywhere incognito.

—C. S. LEWIS

Some of you will understand what I mean when I say, working in ministry isn't always a joyride. That is why I have found the Conversation with Jesus activity especially vital. The waters can get pretty choppy when people are under stress and bandy about religious justifications for their mistreatment of others. When people behave this way toward me, many times they dismiss their conduct with something to the tune of, "He's brought this on himself because he's flat-out wrong about _____," or "He deeply offended me by _____." (Here is where I practice Quieting to Connect). Real or imagined by others, these incidents drive me to Jesus for perspective and the reassurance of His presence.

Once, I had three different women upset with me at the same time. Typically, I'm not an overly sensitive guy. I knew Jesus would have something to say about my feelings, so I took them—and these three—to Him. Apparently, He saw me coming.

"Lord," I asked, "how would you like to talk to me about this situation?"

"Oh . . . my wounded daughters," He said. After a long and compassionate pause, He continued, *"They've spent their lives searching for validation—especially, looking for a man who would validate them."*

"Lord, by your tone I can tell you have compassion for them," I said, trying to hide my disbelief. Wasn't He on *my* team? "I have nothing but frustration when I think about those three. They are making my life miserable!"

"Ed," Jesus said gently, *"they are trying to live up to an image of themselves that I did not create."*

"But what about their anger? It may be passive, but it hangs over every interaction we have. I feel their loathing. Why me?!" I pouted.

"I know. I can see how hard they are on you. Unfortunately (or fortunately, in My book), you are in a place of authority. Because they don't interact well with men, you have become their target. It's like a dance. Your consistent kindness toward each of them has made these women feel less afraid or intimidated by you than other men. Their anger helps them maintain a safe distance. The closer they move and allow themselves to get to you, the more fears get stirred up inside."

"Okay, Lord. So what do I do?" I asked.

His voice softened as He answered, *"Just remember that they are My wounded daughters. Remember they are Mine, Ed. Love my daughters for My sake."*

As soon as He finished speaking, Luke 6:35 (ESV) entered my thoughts: "Love your enemies . . . expecting nothing in return."

I hope you notice, God didn't tell me to repent or go to the cross. That was it. Somehow, in the days and months following, His strength enabled me to avoid judging the trio. Then, about three months later, one of the women had an incredible breakthrough with Jesus. During a Face of Grace activity at a leader training class, Carol discovered her own face of grace. Consistent experiences of being treated as special and favorite empowered her to put down her anger and move more fully in the freedom of her true, grace-based identity. Today, Carol is a whole different person. If I hadn't talked the situation over with Jesus, I would never have experienced the blessing of seeing her through His eyes—the transformation could never have happened for either of us.

Activity #6: Conversation with Jesus

The Conversation with Jesus activity is designed to help us develop an awareness of His presence and, subsequently, to engage intentionally with Him throughout each day. Moment by moment, day by day, Immanuel is always with us. Truly, the Lord is ever present. In Matthew 1:23, the angel proclaimed Jesus' name would be called "'Immanuel,' (which means 'God with us')." The Bible testifies that this is the life Jesus modeled with His Father. From His own lips, Jesus said He only did what He saw the Father doing, and only spoke the things He heard His Father saying (John 5:19). It is this "with-ness" and guidance that Conversation with Jesus makes room for in our lives.

WHERE IS THIS PRACTICE DEMONSTRATED IN THE BIBLE?

Keep in mind, more than once this same Savior promised that He would always be with us (Matthew 28:20). Always. And for what? As His time on Earth was drawing to a close, Jesus reassured His followers that the Holy Spirit would remain—living in us and guiding us into all Truth (John 16:13). Whether or not we are always aware, He is near.

Throughout the New Testament, we read about people *conversing* with Jesus at the same time they were oblivious to who He was; technically, they were *with* Jesus but unaware of His presence. Mary didn't take the gardener at the tomb to be Him, just as the disciples on the Emmaus Road were blind to their fellow traveler's identity.

Cultivating an awareness of His presence and the ability to carry on a conversation with Him is a normal part of a biblical lifestyle. Paul demonstrated it in his first letter to the Church at Corinth. Addressing many of their questions, Paul was able to discern the difference between his own opinions and the Lord's answer on a given topic.

If it could happen with Mary, the Emmaus Road pair, and Paul, certainly this kind of sacred, two-way conversation can—and should—happen with us. Let's be honest enough to admit the probability. You and I are busy, after all, and the distractions of life make it easy to forget that God is right there by our side. His creation, His Word, and our circumstances all speak! The kind of discernment we are after is only possible through intentional, disciplined practice with Jesus. That is why, at any given moment, we are wise to consider:

- Am I living like Jesus is with me?
- Have I been in constant interaction with Him today?
- What percentage of my day have I been engaged with Him?

Recalling our experiences with the Lord is scriptural—and essential! To be clear, when Conversing with Jesus, you and I aren't just talking to ourselves or yakking at some divine drive-through squawk box. Rather, we are inviting a vibrant, two-way conversation with Immanuel.

Using the template of the Conversation with Jesus activity, we question, we listen, God answers. Even when He may seem silent, rest assured, He has not left us alone. Fear and trauma can make this difficult for some. Such individuals should be encouraged to continue the practice of Scripture Reflection (chapter 9), strengthening their ability to engage with God until they feel ready to revisit this activity. With practice and healing, our capacity will build. Holding high expectation and low pressure, each of us can learn to pay attention to whatever Scripture, thoughts, feelings, memories, impressions, or symbols that the Holy Spirit may bring to mind. By regularly practicing this activity, we will become accustomed to engaging everyday life in a with-God way. The more we do, the more we will begin to recognize that His vision of a situation is often very different than our perception. Learning to recognize Jesus' presence in real-time will transform our reality.

(Note: The remainder of this chapter is written as directions for small group leaders. These directions will help guide your group through a series of interactive questions.)

GROUP LEADER INSTRUCTIONS

1. To begin

    To begin, complete either the Growing Gratitude activity (chapter 5) or the Jesus Moments and Jesus Stories activity (chapter 6) before diving into this new activity. Why? As with other things we have learned, it is important to help group members individually establish and reaffirm a solid relational bond with Jesus. Once this connection is firm, it is time to begin something new.

2. Share, pray, and provide instructions.
    - Share your personal reflections on the previous activity.
    - Offer a brief prayer. The exact words are not important; however, their sequence is. Generally, the prayer goes something like this: "Jesus, we're thankful that You are always with us. There is never a moment that You forget us, and You always want to connect with us to know Your heart, life, love, and grace. Help us experience Your presence and peace as we seek to connect (engage, talk, etc.) with You. I pray that You

silence every voice here that is not Yours so that we may listen to You and nobody else. In Your name we pray, amen."

- Provide your group with the following instructions before beginning the Conversation with Jesus activity:

  ○ The purpose of the exercise is to connect with Jesus and enjoy His presence.

  ○ During the activity, maintaining a sense of gratitude and an awareness of His presence is key. If you lose this awareness, return to your Gratitude Moment or Jesus Story (depending on which activity your group previously completed). Once you regain your sense of gratitude or a sense of Jesus' presence, you can resume asking questions.

  ○ Get comfortable. Sit or lie down if you'd like. You can participate either with eyes open or closed (for many people, closing their eyes helps them avoid becoming distracted).

  ○ As your group leader, I will be posing a progression of questions and providing instructions throughout. Getting used to conversational interaction with Jesus is more important than the questions themselves.

  ○ I invite you to personalize each question—asking Jesus for yourself. You're invited to join us. If you'd rather not, it's fine. Just continue reflecting on your Gratitude Moment or Jesus Story.

  ○ Once I've asked each question, silently ask the question to Jesus for yourself, and then await His response. Remember: His response may come in the form of thoughts, memories, impressions, pictures, scriptures, etc., that come to mind. Pay attention to His leadership.

      ◦ If you would like, you may journal your impressions as we go.

      ◦ You will have twenty seconds between questions to interact with Jesus. The interactive part of this activity will take about five to seven minutes.

3. Revisit God's presence.

Now that you've given your group an overview, they should be ready to go. Ask them to close their eyes and invite God's presence by revisiting their Gratitude Moment or Jesus Story once again. Stir their remembrance by asking the following questions:

- What was happening in that moment?
- What did this memory feel like emotionally? What did it feel like physically?
- What was it like to feel gratitude and Jesus' presence? What was it like to be with Him?
- If you want to thank Him for that moment, do that.

4. Lead questions for conversing with Jesus.

As you move into the interactive questions, remind group members that they are welcome to open their eyes or keep them closed. You will be directing them through four movements: Attachment with Jesus, His Consistent Presence, His Heart for Me, and My Response to Him. As the Lord leads you, choose one or two questions from each movement to pose to your group.

Movement 1: Attachment with Jesus

These questions are meant to introduce participants to a fresh sense of His delight in being with them. Each relates to individual bonding and attachment with the Lord.

- *Jesus, do You love me?* (Pay attention to thoughts, feelings, memories, impressions, scriptures that may come to mind.)
- *Jesus, why do You love me?*
- *Jesus, am I really Your special and favorite?*
- *Jesus, when You look at me through Your eyes of grace, what do You see?*

Movement 2: His Consistent Presence

It is important to help people recognize that Jesus is—and always has been—with them. Questions in this section address this as well as issues surrounding the joy God takes in each of us.

- *Jesus, on the day I was born, what was the first thought You had about me?*
- *Jesus, when I opened my eyes this morning, what were You thinking about me?*
- *How do I bring You joy?*
- *Is there something You really like doing with me, Lord?*
- *Jesus, sitting here right now in this room, what are You thinking about me?*

Movement 3: His Heart for Me

This section gives Jesus the opportunity to share His heart with participants in the moment.

- *Jesus, is there anything You'd like to say to me?*
- *Is there anything You'd like me to do, Lord?*
- *Why is this important for me to know now, Jesus?*

Movement 4: My Response to Him

When you are finished asking questions from the first three movements, finish with these.

- Is there anything you want to say to Jesus?
- Is there anything you would like to thank Him for? (Pay special attention to what that sense of thanksgiving feels like emotionally and physically.)

5. Process the experience together.

To wrap up your experience Conversing with Jesus, acknowledge that sometimes the activity can feel awkward—especially if group members are new to it or if they feel like they need more time or practice. Be sure to affirm that this will get better over time as they practice.

As with the Scripture Reflection activity, we want to improve our ability to experience God's presence and discern His voice. For that reason, it is a good idea to remind people about the Right-of-Way Rules of the relational road, which we reviewed in chapter 9.

When deciding how you'd like to structure this, consider the size of your group. Do you want to keep everyone together or break into groups of three? Depending on the personalities in the room, you may want to ask for volunteers to share or pose specific questions.

6. Conclude with praying with Jesus for one another (See Chapter 8, Joining with Jesus activity).

Much of what is shared in this activity is very personal. You and your group members will have been given access to vulnerable places in each other's hearts and minds. An impactful way to conclude your time is by Joining with Jesus in prayer for one another.

FINAL THOUGHTS

Be aware that not everyone can readily do this activity. For instance, some really cannot come up with a Jesus Story if they are new Christians or something has triggered them. That is why activities found in chapters 5, 6, and 7 are essential to the whole process. Jesus' presence must be central.

As you work your way through the four movements for Conversation with Jesus, tailor it to your group. I recommend you use all questions listed in Movement 1, select one or two questions in Movements 2 and 3, and finish by asking all the questions in Movement 4. (The longer you practice this and learn to stay connected with Jesus as you lead this activity, you may begin to discern and formulate original questions for your group to consider in the two middle movements.) Remember, it is the sequence of the Conversation with Jesus activity that matters: we want to help group members connect with Jesus, experience a constant awareness of His presence, discern His heart for them, and have a chance to respond.

Conversation with Jesus: Sarah's Story

The jolt of a phone ringing at 2:00 a.m. startled my husband and me awake. My mom had suffered a heart attack. And the report got worse. They also found cancer metastasized from the liver in four other places. I flew out the next day.

As I traveled, I thought about her life. My dad had passed away two and a half years before, and it had been tough for her since then. That memory, along with one from her childhood, had dogged her as long as I can remember. At five years old, she had been left by herself in the family farmhouse during a fierce rainstorm—alone and traumatized. Her scars left me with an ongoing prayer for her: *Lord, could you please allow me to help her heal those traumatic memories?* Over time, I had tried to approach both events—asking if we could pray for her healing together—but Mom simply wasn't willing to go there.

With Mom lying in a hospital bed, I began a Conversation with Jesus. I lifted these things to Jesus again. I promised Him that I would stop trying to "fix it" for her. This time, He simply encouraged me to hug Mom each night and tell her that I loved her. That was something her mother had never said to her growing up. He continued, asking me to say yes to the unknown that lay ahead for my mother and all of our family. As soon as my heart obeyed, a sense of peace flooded throughout my body. He reassured me that He is a good Father. As a nightly routine, I spent the next several weeks expressing my appreciation to her for the life she had lived before us. Gradually, she began practicing appreciation as well.

Two months and one week later, I got a surprise. Mom came out of her bedroom and thoughtfully said, "You know, I just realized something: Jesus was there with me by the window during that rainstorm. He was *right* there!" A smile spread across my face. We hadn't been talking about it or addressing the circumstance in any way. This was Mom's moment . . . planned by Jesus for her healing. I was overcome with joy at how God let me glimpse His power as He helped Mom resolve this. I chuckled to myself, thinking, *He didn't need me at all!*

Later it dawned on me that my obedience in actively loving Mom and appreciating her had played a part in her healing. Love never fails. That love empowered her to relax and return to that scary farmhouse for healing. God had allowed her to experience His presence so she could know that she had never been alone—and never would be. With that, shalom pervaded her whole being. She was noticeably more peaceful from that day forward. Just about one month later, Mom stepped quietly into Jesus' waiting arms. The last words I remember her saying to me were spoken in a phone conversation just a day or so before she died: "I love you, too, sweetheart."

PART 3

UNLEASHING CREATIVITY
IN YOUR SMALL GROUP

11 Finding Shoes That Fit: Customizing Beyond Becoming Activities

God is not simply saving diverse individuals and preparing them for heaven; rather he is creating a people for his name, among whom God can dwell and who in their life together will reproduce God's life and character in all its unity and diversity.

—GORDON D. FEE

Recently I gave away a pair of shoes. They were great shoes—stylishly versatile, built for all terrains, and *super* comfortable. There was just one problem: every time I put them on I felt like Bozo the Clown. That's because I tried to force a fit. You see, I've got really wide feet, but I was hooked on the comfort and look of this one particular shoe. A friend had told me about them, so I went to the mall, anticipating a purchase. As any good shoe salesman would do, when my regular size didn't fit, the guy helping suggested I try the shoe a couple of sizes up to see how they felt. *Genius!* The width was just right. *Perfect!* I thought. As I sat comfortably in the store, taking in my glorious new kicks, I have to admit, they *did* feel great. Standing in front of the knee-length mirror they looked pretty good too. "I'll take them!" I said. The retailer and I were both pleased by the transaction. And then I got home.

That night, I had a meeting and—as you may expect—I was excited to wear my new purchase. I laced them up, grabbed my iPad, and headed out the door. Walking to the car was when I first noticed it: the extra inch and a half of shoe out in front of me was causing an obvious and awkward change in my stride. Thinking I'd get used to it, I continued on my way. Compensating for my new "flippers," I lifted my knees a little higher with each step. It produced a quirky gate that didn't feel natural . . . but that would come, I told myself.

Later that night after teaching, I stood around talking to people and—yes—those shoes *were* supportive and comfortable, but every time I took a step, I felt like I was stepping off a dock to water-ski. Knowing the return policy was voided once I wore the shoes outside, I made a valiant attempt to grow to love the pair over the next few weeks. Alas, I couldn't overcome the mental clown shoe image when I wore them. So, when my friend John remarked that he liked them, I readily handed them over. (Being his proper shoe size, they look great on him, by the way.)

Have you ever had buyer's remorse? Like me, have you found yourself swept up in the persuasive influence of friends, the marketing enthusiasm of a sales associate, or the convincing sway of the "latest and greatest" solution in any given category? When objectivity is lost, we can often be too quick to buy something that is really not right for us.

When leading a small group, don't wear clown shoes. The most effective leaders don't. If we are honest, you and I know that what may be perfect for another might not fit us. If things don't actually fit, we can't walk around in them—we end up looking ridiculous and may even blister others as our inauthenticity rubs people wrong. To lead well, you and I need to take what we are genuinely excited to share and invite others to step into it with us. *Beyond Becoming* activities and the principles behind *Becoming a Face of Grace* are designed to empower you and me to do just that. Two simple steps are involved:

- Identify your God-given area of interest or passion.
- Tailor the activities to establish and build upon a grace-based foundation for (and among) your small group members.

So, what is your pleasure? What fires you up? Be it worship, hiking, painting, finances, sports, book or sermon discussion, whatever, *Beyond Becoming* activities are designed to be readily "plugged in" around what makes you be *you* as a leader. See what that means? In this context—just as you are—there is an opportunity to express your unique calling, engage your style, and activate your exceptional gifts.

You may have already picked this up from the reading, but generally a good format to follow includes

- Beginning with Growing Gratitude (chapter 5), Jesus Moments and Jesus Stories (chapter 6), or Quieting to Connect (chapter 7)
- Inserting the interest area, curriculum, or Scripture Reflection of your choice
- Ending with Joining with Jesus (chapter 8)

Simple really. It's kind of like building a grace sandwich. The grace-building activities you've learned are the bread that holds your whole group together.

Perhaps a few examples will help. Maritza and I had been meeting with some small group leaders for roughly four years. We were investing in relationships with these special people long before I knew I'd be writing anything. This group vividly demonstrates how grace-based attachment sets a foundation that frees people to be themselves and as a result makes them better, more authentic leaders.

When we got to the end of the *Beyond Becoming* activity training, I asked these friends for feedback. "How can you imagine using what you've learned in your own group? How has it affected your daily life?" Here are a few of examples of what was gleaned.

Going Beyond: Zach's, Isabella's, and Kate's Stories

Zach.

Our group has been meeting for a long time. When you're in the middle of a process, sometimes it's hard to figure out what's happening. I prefer things to have a more obvious cause and effect about them. This has been subtle but powerful. I absorbed it by experiencing what Ed and Maritza modeled. However it came about, as I look back over what I've learned in this process, I recognized how much fear has been a part of my existence. It wasn't a specific fear of anything. Like a lot of guys, I think I have just had a generalized, low-grade fear of my emotions. For most of my life, I haven't totally trusted myself to handle my feelings when they *have* come up with others—especially if they were negative. (I avoided *those* like the plague!)

At the time, I preferred doing life at a relational distance. The idea that I could maintain any relationship amid conflict was foreign to me. Now I understand how God sees people, no matter how they are behaving. Not only is it helping me to deal with my fear stuff, but I have learned what it actually means to be a face of grace with others. I don't feel I've "graduated," but recognizing it is a big thing.

I used to go to a small group because I thought it was "the Christian thing to do." Way down deep, however, I thought it was a waste of time. Now my own life is evidence: you can't become like Christ without community. Somewhere along the way, I sincerely became happy to see people—that's when I experienced the clarity: *I* had become a face of grace. When that happens, I've noticed, people start hanging around. They like you more and you kind of like them more. Walking into such beauty and joy has created a welcoming atmosphere that is a gift to everybody in our group. I'm highly aware of it—especially because we lead a group now.

It's all still in process going forward, but it's an invaluable one. So that everyone has the same opportunity to experience it, we build our group around establishing sanctified, grace-based attachment. It usually looks something like this:

- Everyone shows up around 6:30 p.m.
- Gratitude Moment (chapter 5) or Jesus Story (chapter 6) activity. Before we dig in, we gather around the buffet and give each person a chance to share a Gratitude Moment or a Jesus Story.
- Potluck dinner. One of us prays for the food before we sit down to share dinner. We enjoy catching up over the meal.
- Scripture Reflection (chapter 9). This year, our group decided to go through 1 Corinthians, so each week I pick a passage and give everyone time for Scripture Reflection.
- Joining with Jesus to pray for One Another (chapter 8). Once we've wrapped up a time of sharing about it, we spend time praying with Jesus for one another.

Each week, people in our group come in the door with burdens. My wife, Kay, and I don't always know what they have brought with them or what they receive while they are there. But we *do* know (because we have asked them) that these friends feel like they are seen through eyes of grace when they cross our threshold. The whole group has caught what it means to be a face of grace, and now they reflect it to one another.

Isabella.

Zach and I are a lot alike when it comes to our previous feelings about small groups. Until now, I'd say I wasn't particularly fond of them. In part, the groups I'd been in were filled with people who *seemed* to have it all together. I knew I certainly didn't, so I never felt safe to be myself when we met. But this group is different—it has helped me relax and feel the Lord's presence in new ways—ever since we began sharing Jesus

Stories (Activity #2). Watching others open up taught me how to feel safe in a group. Over time, I truly became excited to show up at Ed and Maritza's house each week! But remember, I didn't come expecting that.

Kate.

I can springboard off Isabella's experience. I wasn't expecting what I experienced. Originally, I came to learn for *other* people. I am a therapist and had heard about the Conversation with Jesus activity (chapter 10) from some colleagues of mine. I was eager to know more about how the brain works to strengthen faith and heal people. I thought I was there for *that* reason, but God quickly turned the tables on me. The relational activities we learned helped me understand *myself* better. I'm more tuned in now. I can recognize when I hit my emotional capacity. More specifically, I don't avoid the feelings of overwhelm that accompany it like I used to. Instead, I invite Jesus in. I've learned I don't have to be strong or have it together by myself.

Though I didn't recognize it before, my life was full of trauma— some of it mine, some of it those who came for counseling. This material continues to bring me healing. A couple of the activities I use most often in my personal life are the Jesus Moments and the Scripture Reflection activities. Now the joy of the Lord and thankfulness companion me. Grace has taught me that the Lord is *always* doing something good— my levels of fear and anxiety are changed forever. By increasing my connection with Jesus, I can offer more of myself to others. As a result, I love Him and others better than I used to. Understanding how my emotional capacity is different from another person helps me remain patient, stay relational, and see them with eyes of God's grace. (Honestly, I *feel* it for them like never before). The *Beyond Becoming* activities have enlarged my heart, my prayer life, and rounded out my counseling skills. I had no idea what I was in for, and I'm so grateful!

12 Conclusion: Leading for Connection

The thing I remember best about successful people I've met all through the years is their obvious delight in what they are doing and it seems to have very little to do with worldly success. They just love what they're doing, and they love it in front of others.

—FRED ROGERS

Working with small groups has absorbed most of my life— roughly forty years. When I first started out, the idea of leading for connection was nowhere on my radar. Still employed as a police officer, I began professional training in the area of addiction and recovery work. During that time, I volunteered at a church in Maryland, facilitating a support group for teens whose parents were alcohol or drug addicts. The group was open and free-form. Kids would just come and talk. For a support group, it wasn't bad. Though my training was good up to that point, it hadn't covered some key pointers about working with adolescents. For instance, the reality is that if you gather teenagers together in this loose kind of forum (without any structure), they will do one of two things: 1) sit in sullen silence, or 2) talk about how miserable things are at home. At this age, their group dynamics don't trend in a positive direction. Throughout the time we met, I struggled to see much benefit or healing result in their lives. Eventually, the rotating shift schedule of my job on the police force necessitated a change. I handed the group off to another counselor—but not before learning a lot.

Six years later, I was ordained and working full-time in rehabilitation and recovery, setting up community support groups near where we lived. There, my "real-life" training continued. Recognizing we are all imperfect people, the place I worked demonstrated a great sense of life and community. The organization had developed an accountability-based model for their rehab and recovery groups. This kind of strict rule is just what most addicts need early on. Things went well in these groups, *so* well that I decided to start a small group fellowship modeled around some of the same material.

Looking back, I'll admit my ideas about how to run a small group were rigid. Well-intentioned but misguided, attempting to bring some of the hard and fast recovery tools into a regular home group setting wasn't a great idea. As a regular discipline each day, members were required to "check in" with themselves using a worksheet for self-reflection. Without exception, everyone in the group was expected to comply. Then, once a week we would meet to pray and listen to how God was asking each person to move forward.

Truth be told, back then I had more grace for support group members struggling with addiction than for those in my small group community who wouldn't stick to the rules. This time—though working with a solid framework—the focus moved once again to the pain each person was in or what was going wrong. (While it is important to talk and pray about these things, these should never be the core purpose of a healthy small group.) Too much structure slowly began to strangle the life out of people. Eventually, both sides of the relational equation wore out—them *and* me!

THE CHALLENGE OF BALANCE

No matter what your setting, an average small group won't function well with too little structure *or* with too much—at least in any sustainable, life-giving way. Balance is a challenge. If you're like me, you've seen how widely this pendulum can swing. Most of us simply haven't been taught how to center on grace-based attachment and, from there, to lead for connection. It is beyond important to find your balance. When the fulcrum of our leadership hangs on grace-based attachment, we become Immanuel centered. From there, the creativity that we share with Jesus will liberate our leadership and grow our groups!

Liberate? you wonder. Yes! As leaders, you and I can model what it means for our groups to treat everyone in the room as special and favorite (grace-based attachment), genuinely love what we are doing together, and freely incorporate activities that will spur spiritual growth and emotional maturity in Christ. That is the beauty of *Beyond Becoming* activities—they are adaptable to what suits you and your group.

THE PRIMACY OF RELATIONSHIP

See the difference? Relationships first! That's our focus. *Beyond Becoming* activities don't tie groups down with workbooks or study materials. They position everyone involved to grow better, grace-based relationships. And don't forget, who or what you and I love most will affect how we behave. Together with our group, using these tools will help us learn to enjoy God and one another more.

When that happens, a notable, positive shift of weight and responsibility will occur. When it does, the group becomes about what Jesus wants to do in the midst of us. Paying attention to this, you and I are freed to respond creatively to the actual joys and needs of our community.

The activities you and I have reviewed are not one size fits all. Try them on to see what works best in your format. With practice, you can rest assured they will help your group thrive. Well engaged, *Beyond Becoming* activities lead to noticeable spiritual growth, emotional maturity, and healing—both for individuals and for groups.

BEYOND BECOMING: BASICS TO FOLLOW

To be called to disciple a group is to guide them toward knowing God and being known—by Him and others alike. It is no cookie-cutter process, but it is made substantially easier if you keep a few important things we have learned in mind:

1. **Be intentional** to see your group and individual group members through the eyes of grace. Your group is His favorite! Each person in your group is His favorite too! Pick activities that nurture this new way of seeing—and being.

2. **Pray for your group**. Refer to the Joining with Jesus activity (chapter 8) to recall how to pray with Jesus for group members.

3. **Have a relational goal in mind each time you meet.** As you plan your time together, prioritize activities that support that goal—setting the stage for connecting with God and each other. Because it's easy to get lost in logistics, orient your meeting around that goal—and not the other way around. For instance, recently our men's group planned a fishing trip on the North Carolina coast. Sure, there were a bunch of details to make it happen—sign-ups, transportation, hotel arrangements, etc.—but Dave, our leader, organized each element around letting the guys get to know one another through conversation. As they fished off the pier, the men shared. After a few days of fishing, the men were primed and ready to share their lives and hearts together.

4. **Personally master the activity(ies) you are introducing**. This isn't a performance evaluation; you don't have to be perfect in

your delivery or execution, but whatever you present should be a genuine practice in your life. If you don't know how to do a specific activity, if it isn't something you're able to be genuine about, or if you know your group isn't ready for it, don't force it. Inauthenticity doesn't build bonds.

5. **Commit to being a non-anxious presence in your group**. As the leader, you set the tone. If you come in anxious or agitated, group members will pick up and amplify the vibe. When needed, engage the specific techniques you've learned to help yourself and group members quiet.

6. **Remember: codependency and narcissism can sneak in to kill your leadership and stunt spiritual growth within your group**. Unfortunately, many small group models that are out there are subtly rooted in these unhealthy habits, yet grace has nothing to do with either. (If you are unsure how to sort out the difference and avoid these common snares, I recommend reading *The Pandora Problem: Facing Narcissism in Leaders & Ourselves* by E. James Wilder.)

BEYOND THESE PAGES

Follow these basics and your group will experience grace in ways that most of us have not encountered in our small group histories thus far. Living as God's special and favorite will daily change you. As these exercises embed that reality in the fiber of your leadership, I pray their immeasurable value will reveal themselves in an easy and wholehearted sense of your true self. Guided by grace, may you extend Immanuel's presence to all you lead—attracting and attaching them to Him in ways that are beyond becoming. May you and those you shepherd grow closer to God and others, eternally and relationally focused on things above. Colossians 3:12–17 summarizes my hope for you and your group:

Therefore, as God's chosen people, holy and dearly loved, clothe yourselves with compassion, kindness, humility, gentleness and patience. Bear with each other and forgive one another if any of you has a grievance against someone. Forgive as the Lord forgave you. And over all these virtues put on love, which binds them all together in perfect unity.

Let the peace of Christ rule in your hearts, since as members of one body you were called to peace. And be thankful. Let the message of Christ dwell among you richly as you teach and admonish one another with all wisdom through psalms, hymns, and songs from the Spirit, singing to God with gratitude in your hearts. And whatever you do, whether in word or deed, do it all in the name of the Lord Jesus, giving thanks to God the Father through him.

Appendix

Is the Shepherd Speaking?

Psalm 23 describes God as our Good Shepherd. Shepherds lead and guide their sheep in a variety of ways—they know his voice and recognize his ways. That means that, as part of His flock, you and I can expect God's personal and unique direction in our lives. So how can we recognize His voice? If we stay close to His grace, we will begin to recognize the following characteristics of any word we receive. Such a word

- Passes the Shalom Test:

  > "And let the peace of God rule in your hearts, to which also you were called in one body; and be thankful" (Colossians 3:15 NKJV).

  > "Peace I leave with you; My peace I give to you; not as the world gives do I give to you. Do not let your heart be troubled, nor let it be fearful" (John 14:27 NASB1995).

  > "I, therefore, the prisoner of the Lord, beseech you to walk worthy of the calling with which you

were called, with all lowliness and gentleness, with longsuffering, bearing with one another in love, endeavoring to keep the unity of the Spirit in the bond of peace" (Ephesians 4:1–3 NKJV).

- Is consistent with Scripture.
- Is consistent with the character and nature of God revealed in Scripture and His people.
- Enhances grace-based relationship and fosters the growth of new ones with God and others. Generally, does not break relationship, if at all possible.
- Passes the Wisdom Test:

> Who is wise and understanding among you? Let them show it by their good life, by deeds done in the humility that comes from wisdom. But if you harbor bitter envy and selfish ambition in your hearts, do not boast about it or deny the truth. Such "wisdom" does not come down from heaven but is earthly, unspiritual, demonic. For where you have envy and selfish ambition, there you find disorder and every evil practice. <u>But the wisdom that comes from heaven is first of all pure; then peace-loving, considerate, submissive, full of mercy and good fruit, impartial and sincere.</u> Peacemakers who sow in peace reap a harvest of righteousness (James 3:13–18).

- Is encouraging and comforting, not condemning.
- Is not toxic, particularly if it is a word of correction. That means, it leads to the growth of grace-based relationship.

- Is consistent with what God has already been speaking.
- Respects and honors God-given authority that He's already established in your life.
- Is consistent with God's work in His people over time and does not establish new doctrines.
- Requires experience and practice: it feels like a spontaneous conversation with someone I love.
- Confirms and/or is consistent with circumstances. By themselves, circumstances are a bad guidance system. But God will often speak in ways that are consistent with our current circumstances or confirm His words to us through external circumstances.
- Is well-timed. God's timing is not anxious, hurried, or rushed. He is patient and His words lead to peace.

(Note for group leaders: we're talking about learning to hear and test what God says to us personally. In this instance, we are not learning to "hear" God for others. God never intends for you and me to take His place or presume to speak for Him. Because it helps each of us grow a deeper relationship with God, the goal is to encourage one another to connect with Jesus and learn to hear from Him for themselves.)

Endnotes

1   Note: Before beginning this book, I recommend that you read my other book, *Becoming a Face of Grace*; it will help you deeply explore the relational foundations of grace-based discipleship.

2   Dallas Willard responding to John Ortberg, Knowing Christ Today conference, Santa Barbara, CA, 2014.

3   Ed Khouri, *Becoming a Face of Grace: Navigating Lasting Relationship with God and Others* (Littleton, CO: Illumify Media Global, 2021), 4–5.

4   Parker J. Palmer, *A Hidden Wholeness: The Journey Toward an Undivided Life* (San Francisco, CA: Jossey-Bass, A John Wiley & Sons Imprint, 2009), Kindle location 615.

5   C. S. Lewis, *Mere Christianity* (New York: Simon & Schuster, 1996), 154.

6   Greg L. Hawkins, *More: How to Move from Activity for God to Intimacy with God* (New York: Multnomah, 2016), 139.

7   Hawkins, 139–40.

8   Robin S. Rosenberg and Peter Coogan, eds., *What Is a Superhero?* (New York: Oxford University Press, 2013), 115.

9   J. Helliwell, R. Layard, and J. Sachs, (2019), World Happiness Report 2019, New York: Sustainable Development Solutions Network.

10 "The U.K. Appoints a Minister for Loneliness," *The New York Times Online*, January 17, 2018, https://www.nytimes.com/2018/01/17/world/europe/uk-britain-loneliness.html.

11 Paul Fieldhouse, "(Still) Eating Together: The Culture of the Family Meal," VanierInstitute.ca, February 4, 2016,

12 Stuart Brown with Christopher Vaughan, *Play: How It Shapes the Brain, Opens the Imagination, and Invigorates the Soul* (New York: Penguin Group, 2009), 5–6.

13   Warren Baker, *The Word Study Dictionary,* e-sword version12.1.1, 2000–2019.

14   Adapted from Ed Khouri, *Restarting Workbook* (Pasadena, CA: Shepherd's House, 2010), 19.

15   Hilary Jacobs Hendel, "Ignoring Your Emotions Is Bad for Your Health. Here's What to Do About It," Time.com, February 27, 2018, https://time.com/5163576/ignoring-your-emotions-bad-for-your-health/.

16   Daniel J. Siegel, *The Mindful Brain: Reflection and Attunement in the Cultivation of Well-Being* (New York: W.N. Norton & Company, 2007), 5.

17   Bill St. Cyr and Ambleside Schools, exercise adapted from "Scripture in Community" exercise in *Joy Starts Here* (East Peoria, IL: Shepherds House, 2013), 32.